Healing for Life's Hurts

HEALING
for
LIFE'S
HURTS

Virginia L. Dailey

BROADMAN PRESS
Nashville, Tennessee

© Copyright 1987 • Broadman Press
All rights reserved
4259-17
ISBN: 0-8054-5917-0

Dewey Decimal Classification: 242.4
Subject Heading: CONSOLATION
Library of Congress Catalog Card Number: 87-17362
Printed in the United States of America

All Scripture quotations are taken from the King James Version of the Bible.

Library of Congress Cataloging-in-Publication Data

Dailey, Virginia L., 1920-
  Healing for life's hurts / Virginia L. Dailey.
    p.   cm.
  Bibliography: p. 127
  ISBN 0-8054-5917-0 (pbk.) : $3.25
  1. Consolation.   I. Title.
BV4905.2.D34 1987
248.8'6—dc19   87-17362
                                                              CIP

To Thomas Wayne Wilson

Acknowledgments

I wish to thank the following ministers who through their dedicated lives and uplifting sermons have taught me enough that I felt ready to attempt this book: Quentin Small, D.D., of the Center Grove Presbyterian Church, Center Grove, Indiana; Henry S. Date, Robert Amon, and Douglas Garrard of the First Presbyterian Church of Southport, Indianapolis, Indiana.

Contents

Introduction

Have you ever felt that no one could possibly understand your hurt and disappointment? Have you tried to talk with your minister? You may do this easily, or it may take a while to come to this decision.

The minister is twenty-eight years old with a loving wife and four lively children. He listens patiently as you stumblingly reveal your pain, pouring it all out, how your life has fallen to pieces, how you don't know how you can go on.

His kind eyes become glazed as he listens. He pats your shoulder as he prays for you and utters platitudes that sound good. The problem is that you are so depressed and confused, you don't know how to apply his well-meant advice. You conclude that he's simply too young and inexperienced to understand your problems. You're sorry you imposed on his time. Later you feel embarrassed that you were so emotional and unrestrained. How could you have let yourself go like that? How could you have revealed your innermost hurts and doubts? It is obvious that the minister himself has never experienced any real trouble. It may be years before he does. You hope he never has to, but how can he relate to *your* problems?

Have you thought of a friend you might confide in, but that friend also has troubles? You may find it hard to reveal your hurts openly even to the closest of friends. Can you be sure that friend won't betray your confidence to someone else "in confidence"? You wouldn't want everyone to be rehashing your problems at the bridge club or in the locker room, would you?

So you resolve to keep your hurts to yourself. Even your closest friends don't suspect what you're going through. You paste a superficial smile or grin on your face, swallow your tears, or make bad jokes that cover up your true feelings.

But let's say you do have a trusted friend in whom you confide. In time that friend wearies of listening to your tale of woe, and you realize you've become a tiresome bore. If the friend is a woman, it isn't long until she says impatiently, "Gertrude, you need to get your mind off yourself. Get busy! For goodness' sake, cheer up!" Or your buddy slaps you on the back and declares, "She's not worth it. Buck up, pal!"

Then there's the estimable church prayer chain. These sincere, well-meaning twenty or more persons pray for those known to be undergoing difficulties. One tells another and everyone prays earnestly. But do you want twenty church members, some of whom you don't know, passing along your personal problems on a telephone chain? You're far too sensitive and proud to become an object of pity. Haven't you been admired as one who could handle your own problems and direct your own life? You may be a church leader and considered a model Christian. You don't want to spoil your carefully nurtured image of being in complete control at all times, do you?

At the library you check out every book you can find to help the hurting. They bear promising titles like *How to Cope with Anxiety; Conquering Grief with a Sure Formula; Loving Again Is the Total Answer*. You leaf through the index with hope, but then your spirits fall. The chapter headings seem aimed at handling every kind of problem except the specific one you're facing. Besides, isn't your disappointment worse than the author could possibly comprehend and different from everyone else's? Nobody else could have suffered what *you* are enduring.

In addition, these books are generally written by psychologists with beaming smiles and straggly beards. They look as if they've never had a problem in their lives. In their picture on the back jacket they also look about twenty-eight years old. Often their training has been in secular psychological systems, and their advice is unsuited to a Christian man or woman. Sometimes it is advice you would be ashamed to follow because it conflicts with your values. You conclude they couldn't relate to a dedicated Christian if they met one face-to-face. Or their language is technical with a hard-to-remember, surefire formula you're exhorted to apply when you're feeling low. You keep checking back to the first chapter to refresh your memory as to what it means. It doesn't make much sense anyway.

So you find little or no help in these undoubtedly well-intended books. They may be useful to those outside the church, but invariably they are not based on sound biblical principles. Some even denigrate organized religion and personal faith or blame it for the hurts and confusion you're experiencing. You're too hidebound by rigid moral absolutes, they claim. You must cast aside those restraints and live freely.

One good book on the subject of handling suffering is written by a Jewish rabbi, but it is based solely on Old Testament teaching. Where else to look for help? Your small community does not boast the services of a Christian counselor or a Christian book store.

After these fruitless attempts to find help, you conclude there's none for you anywhere, and you're on your own again. No one else understands your situation. You repress your hurt and tell yourself to stop feeling sorry for yourself. After all, doesn't everyone have troubles? All you have to do is look around. The world is full of tragedy. Do you expect to escape the common lot of men and women in this troubled world? God never promised that the Christian would be spared the hardships that others have to bear. Didn't Christ say, "In the world ye shall have tribulation: but be of good cheer; I have overcome the world" (John 16:33)?

The result is that you flounder on for months or even years, miserable and depressed, physically ill from repressed emotions, and refusing to admit that you *are* grievously disappointed and hurt or that you have suffered a traumatic experience which has changed your whole life. Nothing will ever be the same again. It doesn't help, either, to know that in some fellow Christians' eyes, despondency is a sign of weakness and lack of faith in God's providence or to know that some other Christians believe trouble is brought to us because of hidden, unconfessed sin in our lives. When we are confronted with this harsh, unsympathetic theory, we painstakingly search our lives like Job to find the drastic sin that could have caused the hurt to descend upon us like a black veil. We are going through what my pastor calls "the dark night of the soul." How do we, then, heal our wounds?

This book is written for all of you who are disappointed and hurting, Christians and non-Christians alike, men and women. There are myriads of you out there. There are many among my own church. In my various roles at church, I have talked with many hurting people. The book contains practical suggestions gleaned through trial and error, not only from my own hurtful experiences but from those of friends and relatives. I have admiringly watched them coping with situations that would daunt the most dauntless and emerging victorious, going on to lead Spirit-filled, worthwhile lives in spite of their disappointments and, in some instances, because of them. Where I have used names, I have fictionalized them and changed slight details to save anyone embarrassment. But every experience recounted happened in essence to someone I know, or it is one I myself have undergone.

The book does not supplant other excellent books or pretend to be the last word on handling disappointment. It is just another personal interpretation with practical insights to a universal problem. None of us sees situations exactly alike; nor do any two persons react exactly the same. We bring our own emotions, backgrounds, values, and attitudes to bear on what we experience.

Life *is* worth living. We need to keep reminding ourselves, "God is working in my life." We can learn to cope with hurts through determination and the application of biblical principles in every area of our lives. The emphasis is on *every*. If God leaves us where we are, even in disheartening circumstances, He has His purpose for doing so. We are important in His eyes and important in some way to each person who knows us. Our relationship with each person is a unique one and cannot be duplicated by anyone else.

If the book helps one hurting person, it has been worth the writing. After my own first major disappointment, I resolved to write it, feeling confident I had something of value for others. But the time was not right, nor was I ready. The Lord in His wisdom wanted me to ripen and mature. He had much more to teach me.

Now after more hurtful experiences, I trust I have reached the proper stage in my spiritual quest to help someone else. The book is written from the heart to others with problems of the heart, soul, and spirit.

VIRGINIA L. DAILEY

1
Others' Actions

"Trust in the Lord with all thine heart; and lean not unto thine own understanding" (Prov. 3:5).

If you are already a dedicated Christian, this verse is likely one you have committed to memory and recite when you are feeling downhearted. If you are not yet a Christian, then the first important step to recovering from hurt is to accept Jesus Christ as Lord and Savior over *all* aspects of your life, and then begin appropriating the promises of the Bible.

You are now prepared for this essential, childlike trust, and He will begin to direct your steps. He will work with you as you are and where you are. Christianity is the only religion in which you are acceptable in an imperfect state. You need only repent of your sins and be baptized. You do not have to strive to reach perfection; nor will you in this life.

Disappointment and heartache may come to you not because of your own actions or sins but through the deliberate or thoughtless or selfish actions of someone you love. A Christian psychologist reminded me, when I was grief-stricken over a dear one's actions, that we are responsible for our own performance but not that of another adult. One has to make one's own decisions. You are not responsible for the wrong or hurtful decisions of others. Keep telling yourself that. Only they are responsible for their own choices. You must not let yourself be overwhelmed with false guilt when one you love goes astray. Do not let yourself be heaped with blame and accusations when you are innocent of wrongdoing. He has the God-given right to choose to succeed or fail.

And some deliberately choose to fail and bring on self-destruction.

One of the most heartbreaking experiences anyone can undergo is to watch a spouse, lover, parent, sibling, or child follow a path that one sees leading to disaster. We are helpless to stop the downward trend. We may plead, nag, advise, threaten, or remain silent, but the result is the same. The disastrous route the loved one is taking may be one of alcoholism, drugs, infidelity, dishonesty, gambling, or any one of other debilitating choices. It may bring disgrace and degradation only to the loved one, or it may equally involve humiliation for the whole family.

An acquaintance whom I shall call Carolyn discovered her husband had been involved in mishandling large sums of money at his place of employment. He was a lay leader in the church the family attended and was proud of giving his personal testimony on every conceivable occasion. Carolyn did not realize the full import of her husband's crime until he was arrested and tried in a criminal court. He was found guilty and sentenced to prison for three years.

Carolyn, an intelligent Christian woman, was left with two school-age children to provide for. Seeing her beloved husband sentenced to prison must have been a terribly humiliating situation for her. After the initial trauma of finding herself the wife of a convicted thief, she took stock of herself with unusually clear eyes. She staunchly refused to defend what her husband had done. Her forthright response to any well-meant sympathetic comment was, "He knew what he was doing. He has to pay the penalty." However, this honest attitude did not preclude her from remaining loyally by his side during the trial and visiting with the children on visiting days at the prison.

Carolyn continued to be active in the church, ignoring the side-long glances and critical whispers of the judgmental. Holding her head high, she continued teaching her Sunday School class—even though the uncharitable suggested she resign—and faithfully attending services. In the past, she had been an excellent hostess and housekeeper. She made known among the church members that she was available to do housework.

At first, some hired her purely out of sympathy for her need. As word got around that Carolyn was a good worker, painstaking and conscientious—and would wash windows and scrub floors—more church members hired and recommended her to others. She did not have to spend a penny advertising, for soon she had more work than she could handle. By the time her husband had served his sentence and returned home, Carolyn had built a thriving business and had even hired some help. She continued until he found a job, and then she cut back on taking housekeeping assignments except as a part-time job.

Instead of adopting the "poor little me—why did this happen to me?" stance, Carolyn not only became a stronger woman during her ordeal, but she won the respect of everyone who knew her. Her gallantry in the face of unfair criticism and her trust in the Lord carried her through a heartbreaking period for her and her children.

It is hard for us to understand why someone we love will deliberately cause us heartache. We should realize, if we are honest, a hidden or open hostility exists for past or present, real or imagined, offenses. Why do pampered children turn against their parents when they grow up? Why do they discard the staunch moral principles and values they were taught by parents and church? Why will a husband with a loving wife and family pursue a woman of low morals and throw away his reputation? Or a woman with a devoted, hardworking husband walk out and say she has to "find herself," regardless of the cost to others?

A man of my acquaintance became so enamored of a known prostitute that he would leave his office on his lunch hour and rush to the tavern she frequented to pick up customers. When she was arrested for her illegal activities, he hurried every day to the jail to console her. His respectable wife suffered intense humiliation knowing that he was being watched and ridiculed by his co-workers. Finally, he lost his job and left his wife and children to live openly with the prostitute.

Why does a man drink himself into oblivion when he knows he is breaking the heart of a faithful wife? Perhaps he has a wavering teenage daughter who desperately needs the guidance of a responsible father when she herself is facing temptation. Only a trained psychologist can explain the true reasons and buried motivations behind such self-destructive actions. Even knowing the probable reason—a deprived childhood, a sense of inferiority, a lack of conscience, a weakness of will, or a death wish—does not console the person who has to cope with the resulting hurt.

Regardless of the motivation behind the other person's actions, the hurting family member must live life as successfully as possible in spite of what is happening. We cannot let other people's degradation drag us down to their level. We must cling to our own principles at all costs and not lose our own self-respect. We must keep our eyes on God and pray for strength to see us through. "I sought the Lord, and he heard me, and delivered me from all my fears" (Ps. 34:4).

After one seeks all available help, the ultimate answer is found in reading the Bible and prayer, laying oneself and one's hurt in the Lord's hands. We must trust that He will give us the stamina to meet life head on. "The Lord is my light and my salvation; whom shall I fear? The Lord is the strength of my life; of whom shall I be afraid?" (Ps. 27:1) is a verse that helps give us that stamina.

God, however, doesn't expect us meanwhile to lie flat on our backs and wait helplessly to be cared for. He expects us to be courageous, to take action, and to make the best of a trying situation, trusting Him to bring good out of the worst disappointments. For good *can* come even if we do not see it at the time. He may increase our patience and endurance and help us to become kinder and more compassionate individuals. "We know that all things work together for good to them that love God, to them who are the called according to his purpose" (Rom. 8:28).

He may help us decide when enough is enough, that firm

lines must be drawn when we shall tolerate indignities and wrongdoing no further. The basic idea of the "Toughlove" organization for parents is built along these lines: tender love coupled with unremitting firmness and resolution. Dr. James Dobson explores this thesis also in his excellent book *Dare to Discipline*.

We must trust that He will lead us in the right direction and let us know when that cutoff time has irrevocably come. For in some situations of hurt over a loved one who refuses to change, a clean break has to be made for the good of others. At times the ultimate and only solution is to leave the cruelly abusive husband, to cut ties with the drunken brother, or to cast off the incestuous father or dissolute mother. The Lord never expects us to continue in an unbearable situation that we have done our utmost to change when the other person refuses to take any responsibility or make any compromise. This is especially true when it is a life-threatening environment. The erring persons have the right to ruin their own lives, but not the right to ruin the lives of others. When we make this crucial decision, God will guide us to sources of help we may have been previously unaware of. Tax-supported agencies are now available for families in all types of difficulties. These are listed in the telephone directory, or a clergyman can refer us.

God may give us the tough courage and backbone to cast out that abusive, adult son who takes drugs and lies around the house, making no effort to find a job. He strengthens us to take a decisive stand when we must for our own mental and physical well-being. Not even a forebearing Christian should tolerate persistent physical or mental abuse. We have to face the unpleasant truth that we cannot change another person. We can only change our own reaction, the situation itself, or both.

Cutting oneself off from a destructive relationship that is ruining one's life is sometimes the only way to proceed. We simply must summon up the courage to do it when all else has failed. Sometimes a firm decision takes more gumption than muddling along, afraid to take action. Also, our pride gets in the way. We don't want the outside world to know about our troubles. We don't want to worry our families when our lives may be falling apart. We hug our hurts to ourselves and try to deny their existence.

A friend of mine with an abusive, alcoholic husband was advised by her minister and lawyer to call the police and have him thrown into jail when he repeatedly assaulted her and even threatened to kill her on several occasions. He kept a loaded gun on hand and would brandish it about. Being a well-known and respected community professional, she was too ashamed to do so. She had visions of the sordid story appearing in the newspaper. For years she withstood her husband's mental and physical abuse until he finally left her. She later said she was fortunate to have escaped without permanent bodily injury. But the years of abuse left her with a scarred psyche. She credits her religious faith in giving her the courage to go on. She says she now feels incapable of ever loving again, and she cannot put her trust in any man. A sad commentary!

My friend Willa had been married twenty-five years. She and her husband brought an eighteen-year-old European girl to the United States, gave her a good home, and employed her to keep house for them. Willa's husband soon became enamored of the girl and ran off with her one night. It was especially humiliating for Willa, a successful guidance counselor who taught a marriage and family course at the local high school. She asked the principal if, under the circumstances, it would be best for her to relinquish the class, but he urged her to continue. Not long afterward, Willa's husband came to his senses, saw his mistake, and begged to return. Willa adamantly refused to take him back.

Whether this was the best decision—Willa was not a Christian—an outsider cannot say. Only she and he knew what had transpired beforehand to precipitate his impulsive action. Willa continued at the high school as a counselor until retirement, but it took courage to do so when even her students knew the story. It also had taken strength not to let the husband return who had hurt her and their grown chil-

19

dren. But she told me that she could no longer love him. It was pointless to try to rebuild a marriage that he had shattered, for she no longer respected him.

And when respect is gone, love rarely lingers. Love for a person who does not deserve one's respect becomes a sick, unrequited love, and Willa was wise enough to recognize this truth. A marriage has to be based on the determination of both to make it succeed. If one longs to be free, the other has no alternative but to let the spouse go. Forgiving one who refuses to be forgiven is useless. A recent book entitled *Women Who Love Too Much* explores this theme of women who will go to any lengths to preserve a shaky relationship, even to the epitome of extreme humiliation and self-abasement. The same criteria can be applied to a man who lets a woman make a fool of him repeatedly, yet he cannot break away from her bewitching spell. Such questionable relationships do not constitute true love but only a self-defeating infatuation. Any relationship that diminishes one's sense of self-worth and demeans one is an unhealthy one. God never wants us to be less than our best.

The most drastic action of another that brings heartache is suicide. A popular church leader and Sunday School teacher in a local church appeared normally cheerful at the Sunday night service. No one noticed anything amiss in his behavior. The following day he shot himself. His grieving wife and teenage children declared they had not suspected his depression, even though subsequently his wife did reveal that he had been worried about oppressive debts.

In another instance locally, the middle-aged husband was thrown out of work by his longtime employer and had not told his family. For weeks, he pretended to leave for his job each morning. He did not even confide in his wife. Instead, she came home and found his body shattered by a shotgun blast, a far worse blow than having an unemployed husband!

Only God knows what causes people to take their own lives, to initiate that final, desperate step. Sometimes the family honestly suspects nothing; in other instances, the person has given ample signs that were ignored or misunderstood. Psychologists tell us that rarely does a suicide occur in which there has not been some warning. Often a family closes its eyes to a person's depressed condition and hopes it will heal itself. That rarely happens, doctors tell us. We accomplish nothing by refusing to accept the truth, however unpleasant it may be.

In any case of suicide, the survivors are invariably left with an overpowering sense of guilt. In such instances, professional help is essential, that of a clergyman trained in counseling or of a Christian psychologist. Again, the grieving survivors cannot accept responsibility for the actions of the loved one. While none of us can claim to be ever loving and wise and tactful and kind, we do not make that fatal decision. The suicide made it alone, whether he was in his right mind, intoxicated, or in a state of temporary insanity. He can be overwhelmed by circumstances, or he cannot see his way out of a pride-threatening situation. Often men thrown out of work contemplate suicide, especially when a longtime job is affected, or adolescents caught in a broken romance decide to end it all. The survivors must go on facing life and finding strength in the promises of a forgiving and compassionate Lord. Even in this most grievous situation, the Lord does sustain us whether our guilt is real or false. He can heal that guilt if we confess it. "There is therefore now no condemnation to them which are in Christ Jesus, who walk not after the flesh, but after the Spirit" (Rom. 8:1). Another excellent verse is Romans 8:35: "Who shall separate us from the love of Christ? Shall tribulation, or distress, or persecution, or famine, or nakedness, or peril, or sword?"

As a high school teacher, I have known several instances of student suicide. Teenage suicide is now rising to alarming proportions. In one case, the young man was only twenty, the beloved, brilliant son of a prominent doctor. He drove his car into a bridge culvert for apparently no reason. No drugs or alcohol were involved. He had been a student in a fine university and intended to become a doctor. No logical explanation for his death was ever made public. In another case, a high school freshman hanged himself in the closet of a vacant house near the school over a girl who rejected him. In a third case, a junior boy had been trapped in a loveless marriage when a girl became pregnant by him.

God can heal all wounds. Presently, we see only through a mirror "darkly" (1 Cor. 13:12). In this world we do not always find explanations for others' actions or God's actions. We do not even understand ourselves. Thus we never can hope to understand another fully, not even those we love the most. As Job, God's great servant, we can only trust and obey and hope to meet our dear ones again in heaven.

"Let not your heart be troubled: ye believe in God, believe also in me. In my Father's house are many mansions: if it were not so, I would have told you. I go to prepare a place for you" (John 14:1-2).

2

Circumstances

"I can do all things through Christ which strengtheneth me" (Phil. 4:13).

My friend Alice's husband died suddenly in a plane crash while on a business trip. He was forty-two years old. Alice was thrust summarily into widowhood with four teenage children. For months she floundered emotionally, but temporarily she was able to live on the insurance and savings her husband had accumulated.

Finally, Alice had to face the reality that she was only forty years old, and she would have to return to work. Before her marriage, she had been an elementary school teacher. After several years, when her money ran out, she did return to college to brush up on her skills and received her master's degree in education. Today Alice is back in the schoolroom, and her children are grown and self-supporting.

For a while, I must admit I was quite concerned about this dear friend. Alice ran blindly hither and yon, torn in a dozen directions, trying to decide how she should spend the rest of her life. She spent hours on the telephone, asking everyone for advice, even those ill equipped to give it, and ended up more confused than ever. She seemed unable to make the slightest decisions on her own, afraid to trust her own judgment. To buy a new car took her months, unable to decide on the brand, model, and even the color. But through this long period of indecision, Alice continued faithful at the church. It took her a while to get hold of herself, but today she is a poised, confident woman facing life squarely, at last standing on her own feet.

Life *can* tumble in on us overnight as it did upon Alice in her secure, happy life. None of us can be totally prepared for the crises that can occur: lost jobs, car accidents, tornadoes, earthquakes, fires, plane crashes, or hurricanes. The only preparation we can make for these unforeseen occurrences is to build a firm foundation, not one of hay and straw and stubble but one of brick and stone. Then when we have to reconnoiter in the face of sudden, overwhelming disaster, we are not cast adrift on wild seas to be blown askew by every gale and gust.

Alice had built just such a stalwart foundation. True, it took her a while to get her bearings, but her lifelong Christian commitment and training came to the forefront when she had to draw upon it. She continually repeated to herself the Philippians 4:13 passage quoted at the beginning of this chapter, as well as other uplifting verses that sustained her and gave her the courage to persevere. "Thou shalt not be afraid for the terror by night; nor for the arrow that flieth by day" . . . "Because thou hast made the Lord, which is my refuge, even the most High, thy habitation; There shall no evil befall thee, neither shall any plague come nigh thy dwelling. For he shall give his angels charge over thee, to keep thee in all thy ways" (Ps. 91:5, 9-11).

Alice brought her four children to Sunday School every Sunday. Today all are active church members themselves and leading successful, productive lives. She can be exceedingly proud of what she accomplished alone.

We naturally ask the question, Why was Alice's husband snatched from her and the children when she needed him so much? Only God has the answer and in His ultimate wisdom, He remains silent. He never explains or justifies His actions to us mortals. In this instance the plane crash was due to human error. It may not have been God's active will for Alice to lose her husband, but God does permit evil to exist in the world. We know that from reading Genesis and the story of the Garden of Eden. It is a world of sin and error because He has given us free choice. "For we wrestle not against flesh and blood, but against principalities, against powers, against the rulers of the darkness of this world, against spiritual wickedness in high places" (Eph. 6:12).

Bad things do happen to good people and to people who lead blameless lives. For us to think otherwise is being unrealistic. I never knew a finer woman than my maternal grandmother, and many tragic events occurred in her life. You probably could recount many instances of similar persons.

My friend Alice's response to her tragedy was totally different from Mary's. The latter had not been seen in church for years although her name remained on the rolls. I called on Mary, a stranger to me, during an all-church canvass. When I asked why she did not avail herself of the fellowship, her manner turned defensive.

"I haven't stepped a foot inside that church since my mother died!" she declared.

"Oh?" I asked, puzzled, trying vainly to remember Mary's mother. "Your mother was one of our members?"

"No, she belonged to another church, but she shouldn't have been taken!"

"Our caring members would have helped you through your loss," I ventured, but Mary remained unconvinced. This death had happened ten years earlier. Because Mary was middle-aged herself, her mother must have been old when she died. Not only was Mary still blaming God and bitter over what was a natural event, but she was unaccepting of His comfort to withstand her loss.

Serene acceptance of what we cannot change is a major step in overcoming any kind of hurt, and especially in circumstances over which we have no control. Mary's unreasonable attitude had cut her off from the ultimate source of strength and comfort. It transpired during the conversation that she also blamed her children for marrying and leaving her "alone," even though she had a husband. As I left, I concluded that Mary was a most unhappy woman. She has yet to appear at church even though the ministers and members continue to call on her. "Let all bitterness, and wrath, and anger, and clamour, and evil speaking, be put away from you, with all malice" (Eph. 4:31).

A friend whom I'll call Fanny lost her husband when he was eighty-six and she was eighty-one. They had been happily married over sixty years. Carl had been ill from cancer for twenty years. The last six months of his life were steadily downhill and painful. On two occasions he nearly died before he finally succumbed. It was apparent to everyone but Fanny, evidently, that Carl could not last much longer.

Two years later, Fanny is still wringing her hands and claiming that Carl's death was sudden. What a shock it was! It was, in a way, for Fanny, like many women, was unprepared to become a widow. Carl had been the "model" husband who handled finances, mowed the grass, took care of car repairs, and spared her responsibility and care.

As her friends see it, Carl was too good to Fanny, too protective. Now no one can please her like Carl. The succession of hired men never suit her because they don't do things just as he did. They don't shovel the snow into the same corner of the driveway. They don't set the mower blades as Carl did.

Instead of preparing to assume responsibility well before Carl's imminent death, Fanny waited blindly as though death would never dare take him. Consequently, she was overcome when she faced making decisions for the first time in her life and keeping up a large property. Fortunately, she has a devoted son, daughter-in-law, and grandchildren who willingly help.

All her life, Fanny has faithfully attended church, yet she has failed to appropriate the renewed strength Christ promised to His own. She is a continual worry to her son and becoming a trial to her old friends, weary of hearing about the "suddenness" of Carl's death. No one denies her grief is real, and everyone has tried to console her, but Fanny is not attempting to face life gallantly, trusting in the Lord's promises to guide her through her own final years.

A major factor contributing to continued hurting may be

our childish unreasonableness and lack of trust in God's grace. We stubbornly refuse to accept that we are also part of the human race prone to sin and error and disappointment. We Christians are not special in that we, too, must suffer the same sorrows that non-Christians endure. Because we are Christians, we cannot expect to be exempt from the human lot of existence or from natural disasters. But we *are* special in that God will see us through our disasters. "Take therefore no thought for the morrow: for the morrow shall take thought for the things of itself. Sufficient unto the day is the evil thereof" (Matt. 6:34).

We have been predestined and forechosen to be one of His own.

In the final essence, none of us thinks we deserve the unexpected disappointments that come to us. If we equate suffering to what we truly deserve, though, we need only remember Christ's undeserved agony on the cross. Rather than wasting time and energy debating over whether we deserved the trouble, we must think our way through on how to overcome it.

Fanny, the widow of Carl, is still involved in intense self-pity, the most destructive of emotions because it solves nothing. Indulging in self-pity is like spinning the wheels of the car and keeping the emergency brake set. Instead of thanking God for a devoted husband who cared for her until he was eighty-six, she endlessly bewails Carl's being "snatched" away as though it had been an act of spite on God's part. This attitude is self-defeating and will never help Fanny confront her grief, much less overcome it. Carl's death could be foreseen and should not have been unexpected.

In another situation, a friend related a strange, true story of hurt because of unforeseen circumstances. A young man out deer hunting with his closest friend was accidentally shot and killed by him. Afterward, the wife of the dead man not only developed an unrelenting hatred for the grief-stricken friend; but because her Christian parents-in-law offered him solace and unqualified unforgiveness, she turned against them also.

Hurting them even further, she refused to let her husband's parents see their only grandchild for years. Her unreasonable attitude has spoiled a number of lives and all because of an unfortunate accident. The young man who fired the fatal shot is still hurting. He says he cannot forgive himself for his tragic error. No one can convince him it was an accident. "Confess your faults one to another, and pray one for another, that ye may be healed. The effectual fervent prayer of a righteous man availeth much" (Jas. 5:16).

Some circumstances prevent others knowing of our hurt. We fail to communicate, and then we are hurt and resentful when no one appears to understand what we are undergoing. Failure to communicate to others invariably leads to misunderstandings. Much hurt and disappointment can be avoided if we are careful to express ourselves clearly, say exactly what we mean, do not employ subterfuge, and try to be sure others understand what we are saying.

At one time I lived in Wheeling, West Virginia, high on a green hill overlooking the Ohio River. Many springs the mighty river would flood and wash into the low-lying houses in the valley. I marveled at the patience and resilience of those valiant souls who, year after year, cleaned up the silt and debris and moved back in. I myself would not have wanted to live down on the riverside, always fearing those floods, but a grim tenacity kept the residents returning to their homes. It was an annual triumph of the human spirit in the face of adversity.

In frustrating and hurtful circumstances, I suggest establishing goals for yourself. Each day plan some accomplishment, if only a small one. Clean out a closet, write a letter to a long-lost friend, hem up a dress, start a good book, or begin an exercise program. Not only set minor goals, but devise long-range ones like sensibly losing excess weight, taking a longed-for vacation, planting a garden, buying a new car, looking up lost relatives, tracing your family tree, or improving your golf game. Goals are important because they give us something to work toward, to look forward to, and to live for. When we stop anticipating each day with joy, we begin to wither physically, mentally, and spiritually. Even a trivial accomplishment can give us satisfaction at the end of the day and a sense of self-worth.

The old folk saying that God helps those who help themselves is forever valid. God gives us the renewed strength to get up on our feet, staggering and unsteady, perhaps, and to take one faltering step after another. If we arise in the morning and say sincerely, "Lord, thank you for bringing me safely through another night. Give me the strength and courage to meet today's problems. Help me through just this one more day," it is miraculous what tremendous power can be called upon.

"They that wait upon the Lord shall renew their strength; they shall mount up with wings as eagles, they shall run, and not be weary; and they shall walk, and not faint" (Isa. 40:31).

Too much rigidity and the lack of ability to "swing with the punches" causes a person to fail to meet unforeseen disappointments in a positive way.

An etiquette columnist recently described a mother who was offended because she was seated to the left of her son at the dinner table and his mother-in-law on the right. She was considering not returning any more.

This is an example of a person so consumed by petty concerns and appearances and so evidently self-centered that she could not accept her placement gracefully. With such an attitude, how could she possibly adjust to a tremendous disappointment? If we become caught up in pettiness, we are ill prepared to meet the great issues of life when they confront us. While etiquette and social graces are important and make life more pleasant, they should never be based on a selfish, self-serving standard. If we are Christians, we are enjoined to place the others' comfort and welfare above our own. A mother who would hold resentment against a son for such an "offense" is one who probably will spend a lonely old age counting up her injuries.

If you are a woman, wouldn't you like it said about you,

"What a beautiful spirit! She is a truly great lady. I wish I could be like her!"

Or if you are a man, "He's got guts! You have to say that for him! I want to be like him."

3

Loneliness

"Behold, I am with thee, and will keep thee in all places whither thou goest, and will bring thee again into this land; for I will not leave thee, until I have done that which I have spoken to thee of" (Gen. 28:15).

Psychologists tell us that loneliness is the most pervasive problem in today's world. We are reminded of this fact around holidays and exhorted to include the lonely in family celebrations. More and more people are living alone, not only the old who may have no choice, but the young who do have a choice.

The two world wars and subsequent smaller wars killed off many men, and women have been left alone all over the world. The extended family exists no longer. Instead of people growing closer together as a result of smaller and widely separated families, we grow farther and farther apart. One author, David Riesman, called us the "lonely crowd." Most of us can count only a few truly close friends, even though we may have many acquaintances.

Many of our so-called friends are business colleagues whom we lose when we retire or go on to another job. Others are useful in social engagements to advance careers or business opportunities. When they are no longer useful, we no longer associate with them, for these were never real friendships in the first place.

We may rarely see former friends we made in high school, college, or in the early marriage years. When we become alone sometime in our life—and most of us will if we live long enough—we feel bereft. There are those who remain single for one reason or another or are estranged from their families.

The lonely also include awkward adolescents who feel rejected by their peers and out of the crowd. Even a married woman or man can be lonely if trapped in an unhappy marriage. Women are lonely surrounded all day by demanding small children who wear on their nerves, and they long for adult companionship. Men feel lonely in business if they reach the top of the ladder and have no one to confide in whom they can trust.

Many good books are available on living alone successfully, although some are written from a humanistic and not biblical viewpoint. They advocate devices for coping with loneliness that sincere Christians cannot accept.

Being alone need not be equated with loneliness. A solitary life is not necessarily a lonely life. True loneliness, though, can cause hurt. Normally, both sexes long for love, companionship, and understanding from at least one other person. It is the most basic of human instincts. We are told that infants deprived of love often shrivel up and die. Adults isolated for a sustained period become convinced they are unlovable and unappealing, undeserving even of close friendship. We forget that millions of others also suffer from unrelieved loneliness and think there is something wrong with us personally.

How can one overcome this particular kind of hurting? I myself have lived alone for a long time and have struggled with the gloomy specter of loneliness. Consequently, I feel qualified to offer suggestions that have proved helpful to me and to friends.

Pets are wonderful companions if you live where you can have them. Over the years I have owned mongrel dogs from the animal shelter, once a parakeet, and always a cat or two or three, many of them strays who seem to find my door. True, they are a care and responsibility and can be a problem when one wants to go away, but one has to weigh the benefits against the disadvantages.

Pets can assuage the feeling of that dreadful emptiness and eerie silence when one walks into the house. If nothing else, they give one a reason to get up in the morning, for they have to be fed and let out. They never reject us, and they understand us probably better than we do them.

One must, though, never make a pet an obsession or let it replace available human fellowship. We should not become foolish over them and bedeck them with expensive doodads and lavish money on them; this shows a lack of depth and true values on the part of the owner. Pets must be humanely treated, fed properly, and given veterinarian treatment. If one cannot afford proper care, then pets should not be adopted.

The night my mother died, my usually undemonstrative cat crawled up and put her face against mine as if she perceived my sorrow. When a human companion is unavailable, a pet is the next best substitute. Feed the wild birds, too. The fluttering of their wings outside one's door gives one the feeling of life and being in tune with nature. They are interesting to watch and identify at the feeder. I also put food scraps on my patio during icy periods, and every winter opossums come at night to feed. They and the cats establish a friendly rapport and sit peacefully together on the patio.

If you are suffering from too much isolation, admit honestly that you are lonely first to yourself, and then don't be ashamed to tell close friends. It's not a contagious or social disease, and you won't be shunned for your frankness as long as you don't whine.

Assuming a mask and pretending with a phony smile that everything's fine and dandy merely compounds the problem. Women and teenagers are especially ashamed to admit they aren't in the social whirl. We like to be considered popular even when we know we're not.

Be honest if you are lonely, for as in other situations, I've discovered that honesty begets honesty. Sometimes others will shyly admit they are lonely, too. Then you have common ground on which to build a friendship. If you reach out to others in openness and candor, they often respond. We all respect sincerity and forthrightness in others.

Not everyone responds, though, for some people truly wish to be left alone. They are antisocial and prefer to remain that way. No approach or technique works 100 percent. If you are repulsed or even snubbed on first attempts to make friendly overtures, try not to take it as a personal affront. Remember that a salesman doesn't make every sale, not even one in ten, and we are trying to sell ourselves. One takes a chance in all human relationships. Keep telling yourself that! Only God is sure and never changes and never rejects us. Count it the other persons' loss if they don't want to make friends with you. They don't know what they're missing when you have so much to offer! Go on to someone more responsive and look elsewhere for new friends. Don't let yourself become disillusioned and sardonic and cut yourself off from the world, not even letting old friends know where you are living.

Go out where you see people bustling about, bright activity, and color. You don't even have to talk to anyone. An elderly friend used to sit in the shopping malls for hours just enjoying the people passing by. Watching others and smiling at their amusing foibles and odd attire helps get your thoughts off your own loneliness and self-pity.

This isn't to suggest you must be on a continual merry-go-round of hectic, meaningless activities just to avoid solitude at any costs. But try to get out of the house among others at least once a week if your health permits. Attend church activities. Be a cheerful participant and keep grumbles and complaints to yourself. Too many solitary people of both sexes grow sour and critical. Go to Sunday School or to small groups where you'll meet more people than sitting alone in a pew in the worship services, although it is important to be there also.

For women especially, don't be afraid or embarrassed to go places alone. Being unescorted is not a social disaster in these days. Women friends are pleasant to have, but you don't always have to go in pairs. An attractive man told me that women always surrounded by other women frighten off a man who might ask them for a date.

One woman I know would not let her husband become a deacon because he would have to usher, and she refused to sit alone in church. Don't be that way. It reveals a basic immaturity and poor self-concept. What will she do if she is left a widow?

It's not a disgrace to be solitary, merely a circumstance. Rise above it. Look comfortable with yourself. Don't slide down in the seat so no one can tell you're alone. Sit up straight and smile pleasantly at those around you.

Of course, women going out alone must choose decent places and restaurants where a respectable woman would not be afraid to be seen. The woman who goes alone to a disreputable tavern or singles' bar has only herself to blame if she runs into problems. A lone woman must use common sense and discretion, not only in her manner but in the type of clothing she wears.

We all know that men have more options and can seek female companionship more readily than women. But men can also feel lonely and rejected, especially if they have tried to date women and not had much success. Frequently they set their goals too high or are not content with a woman near their own age or not of movie star caliber. That plainer, less scintillating girl can turn out to be a wonderful companion and sure antidote to rejection.

Whether man or woman, if you are alone, do plan enjoyable outings each week—something you'll enjoy: a concert, play, lecture, or sports event. There is nothing unchristian or necessarily frivolous about pleasing oneself for pure enjoyment, as long as it doesn't take precedence over duties and doesn't deplete one's purse. The concept from our Puritan heritage that a Christian should always be somber is a false one. Even Christ attended wedding parties. Remember His changing water into wine at the wedding feast at Cana?

So do get out among others if you are lonely. Observe what's going on around you. Above all, look at ease with yourself. I always take a book with me, and if nothing else,

I read. Don't hide in corners or hover behind pillars. If you aren't comfortable with yourself, who else is going to be? Persons lacking poise and self-assurance rarely attract others because they subtly transmit their uneasiness and uncertainty. Your self-confidence helps break down barriers, and often some will speak to you, perhaps someone in the same boat as you. You gain your self-confidence by continually reminding yourself that you are precious in God's eyes.

If no one speaks to you, enjoy yourself anyway. If you are invited to a social gathering, look genuinely interested in others and encourage them to talk about themselves: everyone's favorite topic. They'll go home thinking what a stimulating conversationalist you were.

Dress up, for it's therapeutic to look one's best. Too many loners, both men and women, get careless about their appearance and grow sloppy. They think no one else notices how they look, so they lose interest in themselves. Older men wear soiled, spotted clothing; women, clothes out of fashion. Always take pride in your appearance. It reveals your self-image and says something positive about you. Look well even to go to the grocery store. You never know whom you might meet there, and one negative impression is long lasting.

I remember a neighbor whom my mother admired because wherever she went, she looked well groomed and immaculate; she always wore short, snow-white gloves when they were fashionable. I was just a child, but I can see her yet walking down the street looking so attractive. Wouldn't she be surprised to know what an impact she made on one little girl so that I'm writing of her years later?

Another antidote to loneliness is travel. I had always longed to take a trip to Europe to enrich my teaching. Because I had majors in English and Latin, I especially wanted to see the British Isles, Rome, and Athens. When I was bordering on middle age, I made up my mind that it was now or never.

After studying maps and marking the places I wanted to see, I embarked on an exciting adventure. I traveled for three weeks alone around Holland and the British Isles on my first trip outside the United States. What a thrilling time I had! True, a traveling companion would have been preferable, but I didn't have one, so why not enjoy myself alone? I looked friendly, asked directions, and talked to people on trains, buses, and planes. I especially enjoyed talking to teenagers and asking them questions about their schooling.

Since then I've traveled widely, occasionally on conducted tours, but the most memorable trip was that first one taken alone. There are certain advantages one discovers in traveling alone, such as going where one wants when one wants and not being annoyed by obnoxious fellow travelers.

While I have walked in strange cities, I kept reminding myself a guardian angel was at my shoulder watching over me, and I was trusting in the Lord's care. "Be strong and of good courage; be not afraid, neither be thou dismayed: for the Lord thy God is with thee whithersoever thou goest" (Josh. 1:9). This is one of my favorite verses, posted by my typewriter, and it stayed in mind all the way.

I was convinced then, as now, that God had a purpose for my life. I was under His eternal care and vigilance whether I was on the canals of Holland, the Acropolis in Greece, or at home in Indiana.

One has to be willing to take a few chances in life, or it can become a dull routine in the same daily ruts. "Nothing ventured, nothing gained" is a good adage. However, one has to be sensible, also. With the current wave of terrorism, we would be wise not to plan trips into certain areas and to avoid tremendous risks.

Another time I drove from Indianapolis, Indiana, to a week's religious conference in Massanetta Springs, Virginia. It was the first time I had driven a long distance alone. But I had seen other brave women out on the roads. If they could do it, I could! I was a member of the AAA and had my car carefully checked before I started out.

The conference was a tremendous spiritual experience where I not only heard internationally known ministers and fine music but met Christians from all over the United

States and even overseas. Certainly worth taking a chance for, wouldn't you agree?

A third inspirational trip was to a seminar for ministers and laypersons at the University of Edinburgh, Scotland. I was the only woman there alone and the only representative from Indiana. Another rewarding experience—one to be treasured—occurred when I heard the magnificent author, theologian, and chaplain to the queen in Scotland, James Stuart, preach. True, one leaves with a few qualms and approaches strangers with a little trepidation, wondering if one will be accepted. But I have found that people are generally kind and welcoming. I must emphasize, though, that one dare not be pushy or brazen. A friendly, unpretentious manner helps to win new friends. If we proceed slowly and patiently, then others tend to open up and include us.

Next, don't be shy about entertaining in your home. Have people in for meals. An unmarried colleague entertained the whole English Department in his home. He bought food at the delicatessen and set a good table. He was a gracious host. Cordiality and warm hospitality, not the furnishings, are what count. Most people feel flattered when they are invited to partake of a meal in one's home. Do invite newcomers to the church or community. Hospitality is one gift of service you can give to your church whether you're one of a couple, a man, or a woman alone. If you're not up to preparing a full meal for a group, serve light refreshments. You'll find that people love the opportunity to get together just to talk. Stimulating conversation is enjoyed by both men and women, and in these days of television, too little heard.

Because you live alone, you need not be reluctant to entertain. Too many of us single people are invited to others' homes, take the entertainment for granted, and feel we are not expected to reciprocate in any way. Both men and women must fulfill social obligations and do their part as much as the busy married woman who generously included us. She, too, will enjoy putting her feet under someone else's table and not having to prepare a meal and wash dishes for once. Men can reciprocate by taking friends to restaurants if they have no suitable place to entertain. To maintain and nourish friendships we must exert some effort. We should not expect special privileges because we're solitary. We must avoid the temptation to trade on others' sympathy and generosity.

A word of advice gleaned from experience. Don't just invite those other lonely souls like yourself when you decide to throw a party. While it's kind to include them, occasionally invite others also. Mix up your groups and look for individuals from different walks of life.

Another way of assuaging loneliness is to make your spare bedroom available when visiting missionaries come to the church or attend conferences in your area. You meet some fine, new people this way and extend your knowledge of what is going on in the Christian world. I myself have kept college students overnight from various campus ministries, another rewarding experience. And who knows? "Be not forgetful to entertain strangers: for thereby some have entertained angels unawares" (Heb. 13:2).

For you retired men and women, if you have free time and are able, offer your services to the church and to volunteer organizations. All kinds of jobs need to be filled: envelopes to be stuffed, dishes to be washed, books to be dusted, and driving to be done. Don't be too proud, either, to do menial tasks. Even if you have a Ph.D. in advanced anthropology and a genius IQ or were a top executive, you're not too superior to pitch in where needed. You meet others in such tasks and friendships, or at least acquaintanceships, can develop.

Be dependable, too. Appear when you say you will, and be on time. For some inexplicable reason, church members seem especially prone to lack of punctuality. They arrive huffing and puffing, declaring how rushed they are, forgetting that those who were punctual are probably as busy as they. Too many volunteers consider themselves free agents, and it makes no difference when they come or if they show up at all.

If you make a commitment, honor it. Build a reputation for being reliable and willing to dig in. This is not to say you must do every single thing asked and be a whirling dervish with a spoon in every pudding. It's permissible and necessary occasionally to say a firm *no*, but be willing to help when you can. "Knowing that of the Lord ye shall receive the reward of the inheritance: for ye serve the Lord Christ" (Col. 3:24) is a verse that should govern all our attitudes and activities.

Volunteering is far less lonely and more satisfying than interminable watching of trashy soap operas, inane game shows, or repetitious sports events on television. If you're helping to cook dinner or set tables for a community dinner at Thanksgiving, you don't have time or energy to dwell on your own loneliness. And what fun it is to be part of a cheerful group preparing those tasty dinners! A lot of laughter and jollity brighten the spirits of the most depressed and lonely.

Another Christian duty both women and men should assume is calling on the sick and housebound. Harassed ministers will appreciate our help, for they have trouble getting around to everyone who expects a personal visit. The deacons in our church provide an appreciated service by taking tapes of the Sunday morning service to the housebound. Even those with families are often lonely.

I visited a woman with a formerly prominent, sick husband. Their son was one of the city's civic leaders. One would expect they would have a multitude of visitors, but it turned out few came. The son was so involved with civic duties that he rarely had time to visit his aging parents. They were lonely and felt neglected, for many of their former friends were incapacitated or had died. While they were justly proud of their son's renown, they would have enjoyed more of his presence.

A word of caution, though. When you visit, don't just pop in and then overstay your welcome. If possible, let the person know beforehand you're coming. Who among us has not been embarrassed by unexpected callers? When my father died, my minister dropped in soon after the funeral for a consolation call. Smack in the middle of the living room rug lay a huge soupbone with which I had treated my dog that day. The tactful minister averted his eyes and pretended not to notice, but my eyes were glued on it.

It is important not to wear people out physically or mentally. A visit of not more than fifteen minutes is sufficient if the person is ill. We forget that elderly or ill persons tire easily. My mother when ill had well-meaning visitors who stayed several hours. On a few occasions, I was afraid she would collapse before they left, satisfied they had done their Christian duty. She appreciated their coming but wished they had left sooner. One must be sensitive to the situation and the condition of the patient. And of course, one doesn't barge in if there is a "No visitors" sign.

Several years ago, an old friend of my mother's entered a retirement home. Out of respect for Mother, who was by then housebound, I called on Mrs. Campbell, whom I had never met even though I had heard of her for many years. From the moment I stepped in to the moment I stepped out, an hour later, she talked incessantly, never stopping for breath. She was a lively old lady, dressed to the teeth. I was able to sandwich in only one brief question that Mother had wanted me to ask. I left literally gasping for breath.

On subsequent visits, Mrs. Campbell repeated the same stories in the same nonstop manner. One could excuse this garrulousness because of her advanced age. But was it any wonder that her relatives rarely visited? One adamantly refused to go near her aunt because of her tiresomeness. What a pity for all concerned!

If you are the lonely one and someone calls on you, let the visitor do some of the talking. At all costs, avoid being a boring monologist. Refrain from launching onto the trapped guest with a recital of ailments and long-winded reminiscences about persons the visitor doesn't know. It is not only women who do this sort of thing, either. Men need to watch their conversations also. They can be as tiresome as women, even though they may deny it. Some elderly men become blunt and grouchy, blurting out anything that comes to mind. Then they wonder why they are shunned by former friends. "Only let your conversation be as it becometh the gospel of Christ" (Phil. 1:27).

Christians should determine to be gracious, well mannered, and tactful. Just because we are lonely is no excuse to be an unmitigated bore. A good listener at any age is welcome either as a visitor or as the host or hostess. Too many solitary people of all ages want to do all the talking, I suppose to make up for lost time and having no available listeners. They then wonder why no one visits more than once.

If you are ill and weak, be honest with the visitor that you are able to visit only a short time. Well-intentioned, sensitive persons should not be offended by your candor, and it helps them know how to set limits.

If you want to be liked, respond to what the other person says with an expression or word. I'm sure you have had the experience of talking, the other persons listening impatiently until you finish the last word and then plunging ahead with what they were saying as if you had not spoken. You feel utterly frustrated, don't you? We're all so anxious to express our own opinions, we can't wait for the other person to finish.

A good conversationalist listens thoughtfully and makes appropriate responses even though the conversation may not be very interesting. Dr. Clyde Narramore, the eminent Christian psychologist, suggests saying, "Tell me more." Who can fail to respond to that?

One friend blankly gazes off far in the distance with her mind obviously elsewhere. It is a frustrating experience when one tries to talk with her. She wonders why her neighbors are so unfriendly, and no one has the courage to tell her.

A pleasant listening manner and responsive eyes encourage others. Can't you count on the fingers of one hand the individuals you know who are good listeners, interested in what you have to say? This is a two-way proposition, of course, for no one should be a tiresome monologist, intent only on one's own concerns. Psychologists tell us that nonstop talkers invariably have a deep-seated anxiety they have not been able to resolve.

Another method to ease hurt from loneliness is to be a good neighbor whether you live in a house, apartment, condominium, or mobile home. Old-fashioned neighborliness is sadly disappearing from the American scene. Be friendly and uncritical of others' life-styles even if they are not yours, and avoid being nosy or obtrusive. Take a home-baked pie or a pot of hot soup when there is trouble in the family. Avoid the trite and meaningless, "If I can help, just let me know." Offer to do something concrete if you can, or just do it. Too many of us make idle promises that mean nothing. We secretly hope no one actually asks us to do anything that will put us to any effort.

Let people know you sincerely care about them, and you'll be loved and respected in your neighborhood. Few people can resist love and kindness even in these coldly impersonal times. Too many of us exist in a vacuum with tunnel vision. Call on new neighbors promptly and introduce yourself briefly and warmly. Make them feel welcome. Invite them to visit your church. Take them a few tomatoes from your garden. When Christ was asked "Who is my neighbor?" He recounted the parable of the man who fell among thieves and was helped by an enemy, a hated Samaritan (Luke 10: 30-37).

If you live alone, prepare decent, nourishing meals for yourself, regardless of your age or sex. It's amazing how many lone men and women live on cold baloney sandwiches or sugary cereal, saying wearily it's too much trouble to cook for one. How foolish! We who live alone need to watch our health, so we can care for ourselves. A friend existed wholly on buttermilk biscuits and cottage cheese. After a few months of this unbalanced diet, she ended up in the hospital with a case of severe malnutrition. Make stews and soup and freeze a portion if you tire of the dish. Balance meals, and eat sensibly. Did you realize being well fed makes one feel more cheerful and look better? Men who dislike cooking for themselves can find many prepared foods in the frozen goods counter, although more and more men are becoming adept at gourmet cooking. The days of women ruling supreme in the culinary department are over.

Small roasts can be baked and hearty meals prepared with little effort. I buy a small boneless roast, slice steaks from it—much less expensive that way—cut pieces for stew, and bake the remainder. That way I don't tire of the same meat over and over.

Perhaps eating alone isn't as much fun as having an interesting dinner companion, but prepare foods you enjoy and anticipate appetizing meals. Just because you're alone is no reason to starve or punish yourself. Good cooking is a creative effort, as well as baking, canning, and freezing. All give a lone man or woman a keen sense of accomplishment. My brother liked to experiment with making pickles and proudly showed off the delicious results to his male friends.

I like to look at the jars of sauerkraut on my shelf canned from the cabbage I grew or open the freezer door and see the broccoli, parsley, green peppers, and other garden produce. Some men take satisfaction and gain exercise from gardening and like to compete with neighbors rather than spending a morning at a golf course. A sense of satisfaction does wonders for our morale, especially when we are hurting from loneliness. We need to know that we are performing worthwhile tasks, if only for ourselves.

Hurt can result from a change of life-style. After a divorce from my husband of twenty-two years, I returned to the city where I had grown up, determined to forget the past and to build a new life. The divorce had been traumatic for me, made harder because I had been reared to believe a Christian never divorced no matter what the provocation. Only a month had passed since the final decree. I was reeling and bruised from the total experience of losing a husband, selling a house, leaving a desirable teaching job, and returning to my home state to be near my family. A further humiliation entailed my return to teach in the high school where I'd taught before my marriage and finding a former student was now principal. At that point I felt nothing worse could possibly happen to me. My whole life had literally gone to pieces. There were no children of the marriage, so I was alone except for my devoted parents who stood at my side throughout the ordeal.

Having been active in a church in my former home, I attended one of the same denomination the day after I moved in. As I timidly entered the Sunday School room, an elderly spinster greeted me, sat by me, and cordially invited me to return.

I confess I had second thoughts about coming back because the lesson that day happened to be on the evils of divorce. The male teacher, a former minister, expounded on the unpardonable sin of divorce for a Christian. No sympathy was expressed for the spouse who may not have precipitated or even desired the divorce. Divorced persons of either sex were immoral creatures; they must seek God's forgiveness and must never remarry. Now being better acquainted with the Bible, I realize there were certain consoling passages he could have incorporated. As it was, there were other divorced persons of both sexes sitting in the class that day.

I sat with my head bowed, cheeks aflame, feeling like a combination of Jezebel, Salome, and Delilah. Although no one knew my marital status that day, I knew it. Later I discovered that one woman's husband had deserted her for another woman; he was a minister. Another's was an alcoholic and abusive to her and the children. A divorced man had learned his wife was a lesbian and had been conducting an affair with a woman she worked with.

Properly chastened for my own lurid state and inwardly embarrassed, I went home wondering if this were the church for me. Could I find the needed solace, warmth, and fellowship there, or would I always be shunned as an outcast? At that moment, I surely needed no condemnation. Now that I was in the unenviable state of being divorced, would I no longer even consider myself a Christian? Had God Himself deserted me in my loneliness and disillusionment? I kept studying Hebrews 13:5, "For he hath said, I will never leave thee, nor forsake thee." I also consoled myself with Psalm

103:10, "He hath not dealt with us after our sins; nor rewarded us according to our iniquities."

That little spinster's friendliness drew me back in spite of my initial shocked reaction. I put up my head, stiffened my spine, scolded myself for being a coward, and returned the next Sunday, determined to make no explanations about my past. God and I both knew what had happened, and my conscience was clear. I told only a few intimates the basic story of what had caused the divorce. I didn't need to justify myself to strangers.

I resolved I would earn their respect by leading a Christian life, as I always had. The church people would have to accept me at face value until they learned to know me. "Herein do I exercise myself, to have always a conscience void of offence toward God, and toward men" (Acts 24:16) was a sustaining verse that saw me through this period.

I am happy to report that that church became dear to me and my permanent church home. But my initial experience there demonstrates clearly how a simple act of kindness toward one who is hurting can influence the future. It may come at a crucial time when it is sorely needed and will have long ramifications. A total stranger reached out when I acutely needed a friendly hand and gave me unqualified acceptance. Today, now past ninety, she remains a dear friend and an inspiration to others with her faithful Christian witness. She, too, lives alone. She must have instinctively empathized with me when I walked in that morning, a shy, hurting stranger.

The impact of only one person's Christian example can be a tremendous inspiration to others, especially to one as needful as I was. How we cope with our particular crucible can inspire someone else, also struggling, to go on. People scrutinize professed Christians to see how we react when life caves in on us. We must remember that when we transverse our own valleys of despair, they can become our finest opportunities for showing the depth and sincerity of our faith.

It is undeniably true that the acts that most impress us are the simple ones that can be performed by anyone. A telephone call of concern, a visit to the mortuary, a note of encouragement, a warm clasp of the hand, an arm around the bowed shoulder—all help assuage despair and hopelessness. We are not so much impressed by the spectacular acts as we are by the small, gentle, thoughtful deeds that uplift us and warm our hearts. A little rekindled spark of hope can set us up and keep us going for days. We remember those who were kind to us years after the occasion itself is past.

When my father was near death and a blizzard had dumped tons of snow on the area, an elderly church member came unasked to my house and drove his car up and down the driveway to make ridges so I could get out. When the call came from the hospital to come at once, I was able to get out and was with Dad when he died, his hand in mine.

Currently, I am blessed with good neighbors, both men and women. One woman appeared the day after I moved in. She had a warm smile and was carrying a vase of lovely garden flowers. She is a committed Christian who has stood by in sorrow and good times. Another, a man who is not a churchgoer, shovels snow from the driveway and plows the garden without being asked. What a blessing good neighbors have been and have enriched my solitary life. They personify in action the biblical admonition to love thy neighbor as thyself. Such kindness and concern are beyond purchase and price.

In social situations, the lonely and hurting face a different kind of problem. In an etiquette column recently appeared a letter from a divorcée who was indignant because she had been invited at 10:00 AM to a Christmas dinner, "if she had no place else to go." The dinner was to be at someone's home whom the divorcée had never met.

Not only was the invitation tactlessly worded, but she felt she should have been invited earlier by this church member. She also despised herself afterward for humbly expressing gratitude for the so-called thoughtfulness.

Having been the recipient of such last-minute, albeit well-meant invitations myself, I had mixed feelings about her indignant, though understandable, human reaction. Once I was called at 12:00 on Thanksgiving Day and breathlessly invited for dinner where they were ready to sit down at the table. It so happened I was expecting dinner guests myself, so I declined politely.

People who issue such thoughtless invitations undoubtedly have unselfish motives. As they look over their laden table, they must wonder what poor soul might not be having a good dinner. As Christians, we should credit them with good intentions, if not for courtesy and understanding of human psychology.

But alone or not, male or female, we all like to think we're included socially because our delightful company is desired and that we'll contribute to the gathering. No one likes to be an object of barely disguised pity because friends want to play Lady or Master Bountiful.

This lack of tact and foresight compare to the instance of a tentative reply when issuing invitations. Recently I invited eight women for a luncheon a week and a half ahead of the date. Out of the eight, two accepted promptly "with pleasure." The others were in doubt and had to check their calendars. One even had two calendars she had to check. Two waited until the day ahead to call. One phoned an hour before the luncheon and canceled out because of a splitting headache. I had to reset the table. All this is typical of today's standard of etiquette—or lack of it.

Invitations extended to single men and women should be the same as for couples. We as guests should be the recipient of common courtesy; as hosts, the same courtesy according to anyone else issuing invitations should apply. An unspoken but subtle attitude says that we lone persons have nothing better to do probably, and our time isn't valuable to us. We should be available to anyone's beck and call when summoned. We are expected to shed our sensitivities and be grateful for crumbs of attention.

Good manners are always predicated on preserving the feelings and dignity of others. Christians should bear this precept in mind. On the other hand, we lone ones need to set aside false pride by being forgiving and understanding. Even if others' manners leave something to be desired, we don't have to respond in kind. To be petty and offended doesn't help, either. It may relieve our tender feelings, but the clearer our consciences and the knowledge that we acted as ladies and gentlemen, the better. "Whoso rewardeth evil for good, evil shall not depart from his house" (Prov. 17:13).

If we retaliate for others' lack of tact and rudeness, then we are no better than they. Tolerance is the best attitude to adopt when we feel slighted and a concession that a slight surely was unintended. We as Christians must establish the custom of considering others' motives before becoming insulted and building resentment. The person always looking for slights and offenses will receive them. We earn what we expect. "The fear of the Lord is to hate evil: pride, and arrogancy, and the evil way, and the forward mouth, do I hate" (Prov. 8:13).

Finally, if you are hurting today because of loneliness, you must not only risk reaching out to others in love but be receptive to their approaches. Some who most complain about a "cold" church are the very persons who repulse every sincerely friendly attempt. It is as incumbent to welcome overtures as to extend them. We are often too proud to appear lonely, so we repel the very warmth and companionship we are so desperately seeking.

4

Wrong Choices

"When ye stand praying, forgive, if you have aught against any: that your Father also which is in heaven may forgive you your trespasses" (Mark 11:25).

You may think this is a strange verse to head this chapter, for we already know we are to forgive others their trespasses against us. If we are committed Christians, we conscientiously try to do this.

But our hardest act of forgiveness is too often for ourselves. We can forgive everyone else and berate ourselves unmercifully. We look back with dismay upon our wrong decisions, poor choices, sins of omission and commission. We dwell endlessly on our past mistakes until we make ourselves miserable and physically or emotionally ill. If only we had done thus and so, we keep reminding ourselves.

We can't drop those hateful errors into the pit of the past and nail a lid over them. We keep dragging them out, sorting them over, handling them until they become threadbare, and reveling in the misery they cause us. In short, we enjoy wallowing in our wretchedness.

Everyone has made errors of judgment, sometimes serious ones that affect the whole pattern of our lives. Failing to go on to college when one has the choice, selecting an unsuitable marriage partner, leaving a job foolishly, loving unwisely, moving to the wrong area, buying too much on credit, alienating friends—the list can be endless.

If we count all the mistakes we make in a lifetime, they could fill pages. But life is composed of trial and error. If we confess our sins, small and large, God will forgive us. If He can forgive us, why do we find it so hard to forgive ourselves for our humanity? We can be much harder on ourselves than He is. God's judgment is invariably kinder and more merciful than human judgment. We are filled with self-loathing and negative criticism. We tend to deprecate the good and positive things we can be proud of and only remember our errors.

Even with the first essential step taken of praying for forgiveness, we may remain depressed and broken-spirited because we must live with the dubious results of our errors of judgment. Whether Christian or non-Christian, male or female, we cannot escape the natural laws of cause and effect. God cannot protect us from our stupidity. If we stubbornly married a drug addict against everyone's advice, we have to cope with that choice. If we did not attend college despite our parents' pleas, then we must prepare ourselves to earn a living somehow. If we left a job unwisely, we have to find another one. The answer is to proceed, not to waste energy endlessly grieving over those wrong choices. They are irrevocable. "Who can understand his errors? cleanse thou me from secret faults" (Ps. 19:12).

Continual rehashing of previous mistakes can cause us to lead gloomy lives. Remembrance of things past can be good and appropriate at times, but there is also the art of forgetting. We cannot change the past no matter how we would like to, but we can learn from it and resolve not to make the same error twice. This is where we show our Christian maturity. We must pray to God for guidance and rely on His leading, knowing He wills only good for His children.

A friend married an alcoholic and suffered for years over him until he died in delirium tremens. Soon she married another alcoholic and endured the same wretched life. Rather than learning from her first poor choice, she repeated the error, evidently not recognizing within herself the unconscious need to be a martyr and sufferer.

We must recognize that, no matter how intelligent we are, we are bound to err, for the choices we made at the time seemed right considering the circumstances. It is only in retrospect that we know how and why they were wrong. Years later we see clearly where we followed the wrong path, as Robert Frost perceptively described in his poem, "The Road Not Taken."

If we only had had foresight instead of hindsight. But to wallow in self-blame over long-ago errors is fruitless. It can only darken the present and the years we have left.

Ecclesiastes 3:1 states it beautifully: "To every thing there is a season, and a time to every purpose under the heaven," and "A time to weep, and a time to laugh; a time to mourn, and a time to dance" (v. 4).

If we are wholly honest with ourselves, we must recognize that it is arrogance and pride that make us so bitter about those wrong decisions. The early church fathers considered pride the cardinal sin. One rarely hears a sermon on pride these days. Instead, we are advised by secular, humanistic psychologists to insist on our rights. We are constantly enjoined to look out for Number One.

Geoffrey Chaucer, the great fourteenth-century poet, demonstrated in his *Canterbury Tales* that all other sins derived from pride, as did many of the eminent classical writers.

We Christians reason thus: How could I, one of God's children, have been so stupid? Ordinary people outside the church do dumb things, but me? I'm special, one of Christ's own. I must have been temporarily out of my mind. Or the devil made me do it, as the black comedian Flip Wilson would say.

We somehow forget later that when we made those wrongful decisions, we did consider carefully all the ramifications and possible outcomes. It is only when things didn't work out well that we can clearly see where we made our initial error. And what may seem in retrospect to have been a wrong turn actually may not have been.

We must never forget that God has a purpose in mind for us from the day of our birth. We are predestined to be one of His own. "Elect according to the foreknowledge of God the Father, through sanctification of the Spirit" (1 Pet. 1:2). We may not clearly see the purpose, but He knows what it is. "Put on therefore, as the elect of God, holy and beloved, bowels of mercies, kindness, humbleness of mind, meekness, longsuffering" (Col. 3:12).

In His ultimate wisdom, He lets us make drastic mistakes. He may leave us in trying situations that sharpen our wits, develop our characters, increase our patience, and ultimately strengthen us. Some of life's greatest triumphs grow out of our being trapped in a wrong choice. A man who did not go to college may build a successful business from the ground up. A woman can be a Christian witness in a job she dislikes if she is conscientious and cheerful. He wants us to make the best of any situation we find ourselves in or take the courage to flee from it.

"Whatsoever ye do in word or deed, do all in the name of the Lord Jesus, giving thanks to God and the Father by him" (Col. 3:17).

This verse brings to mind a janitress who worked in a high school where I taught. She was a cheerful, elderly woman with a bedridden husband. When I arrived each morning, she was on the job dusting the principal's office. We always had a little chat about her feeding the birds before she left for work, caring for her husband's needs, and other such matters. When she retired, she had one of the largest retirement parties I ever attended. Everyone at the school from the superintendent down respected her for her cheerfulness, diligence, and lack of complaints about her cares and duties. She literally brightened the corner where she was.

Hurting over wrong decisions is largely futile because we are mourning over human error, which has existed since Eve chose to eat the apple or fig or whatever fruit it was. Imagine how Adam and Eve felt when they were expelled from the Garden of Eden! Talk about serious errors of judgment! Yet they lived to become the progenitors of the human race in spite of their flagrant disobedience to God. He had a foreordained plan for their lives.

Saul, holding the robe of the martyred Stephen, watched silently as Stephen was stoned to death. Saul continued to persecute the Christians at every opportunity. Yet after his miraculous experience on the Damascus Road, Saul became the majestic apostle Paul, missionary to the Gentile world. What if Paul, after his conversion, had spent the rest of his life wringing his hands and shedding tears over his dreadful past wrongs? Instead he wrote 1 Timothy 1:12-13: "I thank Christ Jesus our Lord, who hath enabled me, for that he counted me faithful, putting me into the ministry; Who was before a blasphemer and a persecutor, and injurious: but I obtained mercy, because I did it ignorantly in unbelief."

King David loved Bathsheba and took her in adultery while sending her husband in the front battle lines to be killed. David was an ancestor of Christ, and we revere and memorize his beautiful Psalms. What an inspiring legacy that particular sinner left for future generations! Some of our greatest biblical and historical heroes had feet of clay and made monumental errors. When they were truly repentant, however, God used them afterward in mighty ways to carry out His purposes.

I always think that if God could work with the haughty Pharisee Saul, He should be able to work with ordinary me.

So He can still use even us with our poor, weak, fallible natures if we only let Him. We trustfully lay our error-filled pasts in His hands, forgive ourselves for our stupid choices, and move forward confident in His mercy and grace, knowing we shall undoubtedly err again and again until we die. That is what it means to be human.

"Let us not be weary in well-doing: for in due season we shall reap, if we faint not" (Gal. 6:9).

5
Rejection

"What shall we then say to these things? If God be for us, who can be against us?" (Rom. 8:31).

Today, we look about us and may envy the "beautiful people," those with wealth, good looks, fabulous possessions, and glamor. We wonder wistfully if they ever have to suffer the dismal hurts and rejections we simple folk do. Surely no one ever rejects *them*.

Rejection, though, can be suffered by all of us, for it comes in many guises. It may be from a parent too busy to tend our needs, from an adult child uncaring of aging parents, from a teacher who dislikes us, from a lover who deserts us, from a friend who betrays us, from a neighbor who is unfriendly, or from a social clique or club we yearn to join.

The forms of rejection are numberless, both covert and overt, and they can affect anyone. Yes, even the beautiful and rich can suffer rejection. Witness the well-publicized lives of Gloria Vanderbilt and Barbara Hutton. Both were called "poor little rich girls," and both hated the appellation. Neither ever forgot the rejections of her childhood. The future Edward VII was disliked by his parents, Albert and Victoria. Victoria always blamed Edward for the early death of her beloved husband.

Hardly anyone can expect to crash into certain social circles uninvited. We may be rejected because of our appearance, sex, race, religion, or background. Laura Hobson's excellent novel *Gentleman's Agreement* vividly portrays the rejection of the Jew in middle-class American society and helped to call attention to that social problem.

Charles Dickens was rejected by the family of his first great love, Maria Beadnell. Her mother, the wife of a bank official, humiliated him by never getting his name right. Charles never overcame those feelings, and they helped form him into the great novelist he became, determined to gain fame.

We Christians may feel rejected by our church where we should feel least so. We offer our services to the Sunday School only to be told there are no openings, or we're too old to relate to young children. We are asked to run for a church office, as I did when my denomination first decided to include women in its offices. After reluctantly allowing my name to be slated to break the ice for women, I was soundly defeated.

We tender a dinner invitation to someone we'd like to know better, and the recipient gives a transparent refusal. We women repeatedly call a friend to accompany us to a concert. She is always busy, yet we note with a tinge of jealousy that she finds ample time to socialize with others. Or our dinner invitation may be accepted, but there never is a reciprocal invitation, and the friendship falters. A man may try to join a lodge and finds he was blackballed. He's too embarrassed ever to try again.

We wonder what is so wrong with us that our overtures are not returned. If we are shy and uncertain about ourselves, we stop asking altogether and withdraw into our cocoons.

Experiencing rejection in some form is a universal cause of hurt regardless of our status in life. When it is persistent and all-pervasive, it can cause us to feel unacceptable in the eyes of others and lead to depression and unsought solitude. We retreat from life, afraid to risk further rejection.

How can we handle this sort of hurt and disappointment? How do we not let those sharp arrows puncture the skin? How do we heal the raw wounds? Rejection of any type hurts. To deny the hurt is foolish and unrealistic. We cannot reason away emotion, or intellectualize it, for it does not respond to reasoning. Somehow, we have to deal with it.

We can either face it squarely, or we bury it in our subconscious to our disadvantage. Sometimes we give up going to church altogether and harbor a grudge because we suffered real or imagined rejection from the minister or other members. For some Christians are less than loving, and they do reject others.

As Christians, we must react differently from the secular world. This is where we show we are dissimilar to non-Christians and where humanist advisors are apt to fail us because they do not understand what a Christian response must be to rejection. We have no choice in the matter, for we are clearly told what to do by Christ Himself.

Hannah Smith's great classic *The Christian's Secret of a Happy Life*, which I recommend as must reading for those who want to understand the Christian, is based primarily on the premise that as long as we hold aught against another, we cannot expect God to listen to our prayers. We must purge ourselves of resentment and bitterness toward those who reject or snub us. We must forgive even if it takes a gritting of the teeth and a subduing of hurt feelings and the all-too-human temptation to retaliate in kind.

"Behold, I give unto you power to tread on serpents and scorpions, and over all the power of the enemy: and nothing shall by any means hurt you" (Luke 10:19).

After we have dealt constructively with our emotions and reinforced ourselves with Scripture, we should consider the rejection as impersonally and intellectually as possible. Perhaps our woman friend did have another engagement. Or she may have been feeling low and not in the mood to go out. Possibly our neighbor had had a quarrel with her husband that morning. So when we knocked on her back door, she wasn't feeling friendly even toward the pet canary. Perhaps the blackballing at the lodge was from only one man whom we had unknowingly offended when we beat him at tennis.

People react impulsively and moodily according to the state of mind and disposition we find them in at the moment.

That is why a friend or relative will snap at us when we have done nothing to provoke that kind of response. Even Christians are out of sorts and low at times. We can't be jolly and cheerful every moment. Experts tell us weather changes affect our moods. Even Christians are creatures of emotion as well as body and spirit. We have to consider the inappropriate response in the overall context of the habitual attitude of responses. We should remember that we aren't always too pleasant to be around either!

Learning to accept rejection impersonally is one of the hardest of all accomplishments, but it is one true test of our Christian forebearance. Timing can influence both the rejector and the one being rejected. It may have been merely the idea or the occasion itself that was rejected.

Yet we cannot escape the painful conclusion that we ourselves are occasionally rejected personally. And that plain truth must be accepted without anger and bitterness. We cannot reasonably expect to be loved or even liked by everyone, no matter how worthy, talented, good looking, or charming we are. And it is ironic that those who are superior to us, we view with unjustified hostility simply because we are envious. Both men and women can succumb to this unworthy emotion.

Meeting rejection is the first hard lesson any teacher must learn. It was vividly brought home to me at the end of my second year in the classroom when I was still naive and youthfully idealistic. I was going to be the kind of teacher whom everyone loved.

A boy I had taught both as a junior and senior was an excellent student and one I especially liked. At the end of the senior year, I asked for suggestions to improve the course. It happened to be one in English Literature and one that I enjoyed teaching. Bill wrote a long commentary on his final exam that the biggest improvement would be to change the teacher. He proceeded to point out my deficiencies one by one as he saw them.

To say that I was crushed is stating it mildly. If the comments had come from an obstreperous student I had disciplined, I wouldn't have been surprised. But from Bill? I shed secret tears but tried not to let his comments influence his final grade. However, I never forgot that lesson. While I evaluated his criticisms as areas needing improvement, I had to face the truth that Bill disliked me, not the course.

Then and there I resolved never again to shed tears over a student's dislike, and I never did. For my own welfare, I could not let myself be hurt over and over. In my career, I had to develop a thick skin and the ability to take adverse criticism, justified or not, if I intended to last in the profession.

With clearer and less naive eyes, I calculated that in every class there were bound to be five students who disliked everything about me, ten who tolerated me because they had no choice, some who liked me, and I hoped one who absolutely adored me! With that more realistic philosophy, teaching became easier and less traumatic when I learned to acknowledge hostility. Some teachers have to learn that some students dislike any and all teachers.

I even learned to evaluate calmly the derogatory notes I received from both parents and students. There were quite a few over the years, sometimes venomous and always anonymous. I told myself I had to accept rejection. Besides, anyone afraid to sign one's name was cowardly. As President Truman so aptly put it, "If you can't stand the heat, get out of the kitchen."

A sense of humor also does wonders for one's ego. A teacher who doesn't develop one is lost, for today's teenagers seem to pride themselves on their bluntness and what they consider honesty. The comforting thought sustains us that the rejectors are the real losers if they are blind to our sterling qualities!

A mother told me a sad story of rejection. Her son Jim was hailed as the greatest athlete in his high school, and he naturally basked in the adulation paid him. Jim was invited to try out for a major league baseball team, his lifelong aspiration. When he departed from his hometown in a blaze of glory, the local papers gave him ample publicity.

A month later Jim slunk back home, unheralded and soundly rejected. He had been cut in the first round of try-outs. His proud parents were as devastated as he was. A resounding blow but one that Jim eventually overcame, although he never became a professional athlete.

A former honor student of mine, and a class leader, confidently enrolled in a large state university. At the end of the first semester, he flunked out and had to return home. When I commiserated with him, to my surprise he said, "It was my own fault. I hung around the radio station where I had a part-time job and neglected my studies. Good grades always came easy for me, so I played around. I have only myself to blame."

I admired him for his forthrightness. The next semester he enrolled in a smaller college, buckled down, and the last I heard was again an honor student. He hadn't let that first rejection ruin his life as many other young men would have; nor did he lay the blame elsewhere for his failure.

We can't let ourselves become rejected too quickly. The answer no doesn't necessarily mean we are being personally rejected, only that our idea isn't being received. We have to be tough-skinned enough to make several efforts. For our own well-being and emotional state, we have to avoid being touchy and overly sensitive. We can't be grievance collectors. We should give up only when we feel we're becoming nuisances. Sensitivity and good judgments warn us when we reach that stage. God will direct our paths.

A friend my mother made late in life was a neighbor with a long-standing reputation for being unfriendly. Everyone had given up trying to make overtures. For months Mother, a friendly, outgoing person who never met a stranger, watched this neighbor working in her beautiful yard and never lifting her head to speak. Mother determined to get acquainted with her.

One day Mother called over the back fence, "Mrs. Adams, we have some delicious green beans in our garden. Would you like some?"

The neighbor did take the beans, but without encouraging

further conversation. Mother was undiscouraged. Not long afterward she called Mrs. Adams and invited her to come for coffee and dessert. Surprisingly, Mrs. Adams accepted. She soon warmed up to Mother's cordiality and the words came spilling out.

It turned out that she was very lonely. Her only son was estranged from his parents, having married a woman they disapproved of, and her husband was often away on business. Mrs. Adams was an extremely reserved woman who found it hard to respond to others. With her characteristic humor, my mother told that she later discovered Mrs. Adams was a spotless housekeeper. Her furniture looked as though it had never been sat on. My mother's eyes were failing by then, but she did notice that Mrs. Adams, on her initial visit, kept staring upward.

After she left, Mother discovered a big cobweb hanging from the living room chandelier. However, in spite of Mother's less-than-perfect housekeeping, they eventually became friends. Mrs. Adams told Mother in all sincerity that she was the only neighbor who had been friendly. Evidently the others, though well intentioned, had not been persistent enough to penetrate her armor of defensiveness and reserve.

A similar friend I made through equal perseverance was a fellow gardener. In spite of her comparable reputation for coldness, I knocked on her door one day and boldly announced I had admired her lovely flowers for a long time as I drove by. It took several such contacts, but finally I induced this neighbor to join my garden club. Thereafter, we often discussed flower growing and exchanged plants. She was another shy, quiet woman ignored by a large family because of a marriage outside their faith. She and her husband had few friends and lived isolated lives.

We must remember that all we meet are not outgoing as we ourselves may be. Some introverts will respond to only the most persistent attempts at friendliness. In the long run, though, such persons turn out to make good, loyal friends. If we can understand why they have become so reclusive, we also can feel compassion for their frequently self-imposed isolation.

The secret is to know when to stop making overtures. Only a sensitivity to the other's feelings and the Lord's leading can tell us that. Repeated attempts may lead nowhere, and the person fails to respond. Then it is time to desist and look for friends elsewhere. We are forced to concede to another's need for privacy and the innate right to be left alone.

Rejection because of our religion, sex, or color may confront us even today. This kind of rejection is based on arrogance, prejudice, and ignorance. Fortunately, in these days of universal civil rights in the United States, we are becoming more tolerant toward those different from us. Television and radio and widespread travel have helped to break down these barriers and intolerance.

We may become a friend to one in a different religion even though we don't share that person's beliefs. I, a conservative Presbyterian, have among my dearest friends an orthodox Jew and several devout Roman Catholics. We can learn from those with different backgrounds and outlooks from ours as well as broaden our experiences and tolerance. We love the persons and take with them their beliefs even if those beliefs are not ours.

A serious mistake evangelical Protestants have made, in my opinion, is to isolate themselves from members of the other Christian denominations and to become too insular. Many of us fail to look for friends outside our own local churches. We hover together and merely reinforce each other's prejudices. We are admonished in the New Testament to be *in* the world but not *of* the secular world. Association with those outside our particular realm doesn't need to contaminate us; nor does it need to weaken our faith if we are well grounded in doctrine. We must be able to give a defense of our faith whenever called upon, but we should not dispute.

The same is true in association with members of a cult who worship an egotistic and dogmatic leader. As long as we know clearly *what* we believe and *why* we believe as we do, we needn't worry about being deceived or drawn into a questionable religion. If we ever wish to win converts to Christ, we have to associate with the unchurched or those fallen away, commonly called backsliders. We can't stay wrapped in little isolated cocoons and ever expect to win anyone to the church.

Another mistake we church members make too frequently is to use pious, obscure religious jargon that outsiders do not understand. We do this to impress others with our piety and religiosity. We show the same kind of insensitivity as when we discuss mutual friends and social events, thus excluding outsiders.

Desegregation in schools has helped to break down rigid barriers between races and cultures and to lessen rejection. I taught in a suburban high school in an affluent community that housed almost no blacks. It was termed the "last white bastion" in Indianapolis. After a desegregation order by the courts, busloads of blacks were assigned to the school, many from the worst city slums, in a one-way busing decision.

A wise and farsighted administration prepared both students and faculty for this monumental change by many types of indoctrination. Now the busing in Indianapolis is hailed nationwide as one of the most successful in the country. The rejection the black students and their parents had braced to meet was kept to a minimum. Only isolated incidents of rejection and intolerance on both sides occurred that were firmly dealt with by the administration.

Another type of rejection occurs in our career lives. Rejection from a job can be a bewildering experience. This is one of the minor deaths that can come to us. I'll never forget my father's woebegone expression when he came home late on Christmas Eve and told my mother he had been laid off. This was during the Great Depression when jobs were hard to come by. You can imagine what that did to our holiday spirit when we were struggling anyway.

A relative spent twenty-five years with a large corporation, working diligently, a "company man," going in early and late in emergencies without extra pay because he was on the executive payroll. He was stunned when a younger, less-experienced man was hired from outside the company and made his superior. My relative was then politely eased out and allowed to resign. His spirit was shattered. He never completely recovered from what he looked upon as an act of betrayal and lack of appreciation for his conscientious service.

Loss of a job is a blow especially to masculine pride, but now that more women are in the work force, they are sustaining the same blows to their ego. Recent statistics report that two thirds of all women are working outside the home.

A middle-aged teacher I knew developed continual problems with students. She was an expert in her field, but she seemed unable to relate any longer to adolescents. She was critical of them, and they responded with disrespect and lack of cooperation. Finally, she was subtly forced out by her principal, but she knew well enough what was happening. She left the profession a bitter and resentful woman.

We are reminded of what the prophet Isaiah wrote in 53:3: "He is despised and rejected of men; a man of sorrows, and acquainted with grief; and we hid as it were our faces from him; he was despised and we esteemed him not." It is obvious that the prophet is speaking of the coming Messiah, Jesus Christ.

God enters the traumatic experiences of rejection if we lay the problem in His hands and ask for guidance and a healing of the hurt and disappointment. One window bangs shut behind us, but a new door will invariably open. We may find a job we like better than the previous one, or we may try something we wouldn't have dared before. Mainly it is our pride that is involved when we are rejected by an employer. If we can subdue that Satan-sent pride, we are one step nearer to conquering the hurt and ready to step out again in optimism and faith. After all, even presidents of corporations and board chairpersons can be fired! And wasn't Christ rejected even by His own townspeople as being merely Joseph the carpenter's son?

Undoubtedly, the hardest rejection to bear comes from those closest to us, from parents, brothers and sisters, husbands and wives. Have you ever experienced being ignored by a member of your own family? Many people have suffered this particular hurt. A relative of mine married a man whose family opposed the marriage because they expected the son to stay with them and support them. The father was perfectly capable of working. Subsequently, when the son moved out with his bride, the parents stopped speaking to him. For the rest of his life, they were estranged, and he saw his sister and mother only once when his father died. In spite of his repeated attempts to heal the breach, the family never forgave him for "deserting" them. When he died, none of them came to the funeral.

An unbelievable story in these modern times? Yes, but it happens all too often that families take unreasonable stands. A friend whose father was a well-known minister in this city was warned by him that if she married her college sweetheart, he would disown her. She was one of four children and her father's favorite. He gave no valid reason for opposing the marriage other than he wanted her to stay at home with him. The groom was a fine young man who became outstanding in his profession. After the marriage, the bride had to meet her mother secretly. For years the father refused to acknowledge the union even after several children had been born.

You shake your head and say, "How can supposedly intelligent persons be so selfish and unforgiving?" Sadly, they are, and the rejections can be exceedingly hurtful to the recipient.

The sisters who fall out after the funeral over Mother's cherry dresser are a good example. We reject those dearest to us over trivial issues. Even though we may be ashamed later, we are too proud to take that first vital step toward reconciliation.

A friend told me that her mother had recently died, and they had not spoken for ten years. What happens to one's conscience in such situations? How should a Christian respond to unreasonable rejection from loved ones? Why is it so hard for us to swallow our pride and make that first move?

If we are at fault, we must say we are sorry and beg forgiveness. If it is the other who rejects us, then we must try over and over to heal the breach and clear the air. Life is too short and fleeting to hold resentments and bitterness for years. Doctors tell us today that there is a close relationship with various illnesses and our emotions. If we clear up relationships, oftentimes the pain in our bodies is alleviated. Mark 11:26 says, "But if you do not forgive, neither will your Father which is in heaven forgive your trespasses."

It is a cliché that only those we love can hurt us. Whether that is entirely true, we do know that rejection by a loved one can stab to the heart. Whatever the reason, no matter whose fault it is—of course, we think it is the other person's—it is our duty as Christians to make the first effort to reestablish the relationship.

If the rejector still rejects us after we have pleaded for forgiveness for real or imagined offenses, then calm acceptance is the only plausible response. God expects us to do our part to walk that extra mile. We are to forgive seventy times seven. When we do and are still rejected, we can be at peace with ourselves and ask for His help in accepting the rejection without bitterness, hatred, or anger.

"Having therefore these promises, dearly beloved, let us cleanse ourselves from all filthiness of the flesh and spirit, perfecting holiness in the fear of God" (2 Cor. 7:1).

6

Physical Causes

"Therefore if any man be in Christ, he is a new creature; old things are passed away; behold, all things are become new" (2 Cor. 5:17).

You may be suffering from a physical handicap or too ill to lead a normal life. Even though I am not physically handicapped or ill at this writing, I have lived close to both of these problems. My cousin who lives nearby has been blind since he was two years old. My mother became legally blind and partially deaf the last six years of her life. She spent the last thirty months of her life bedfast and suffering in a nursing home where I visited daily. I watched my father deteriorate slowly over a period of four years from a debilitating illness. From the standpoint of an emotionally involved onlooker, I can relate to the hurting physical causes can bring to the person and to the loved ones.

The powerful Christian testimony of the quadriplegic Joni Eareckson in her brave battle against total paralysis has inspired millions through her speeches and writing. We all know others who have succeeded over tremendous physical handicaps or chronic invalidism. Fanny Crosby, the prolific hymn writer, was blind. The "divine" Sarah Bernhardt overcame the handicap of an artificial leg. Helen Keller's tremendous triumph over triple handicaps is known to every school child. These are only a few examples of talented persons who persisted and succeeded despite physical handicaps. Reading of them makes us comparatively well persons ashamed of our petty complaints about minor inconveniences.

How can the ordinary person overcome both physical and emotional hurt he feels because of illness or a handicap? For it is sadly true that many of us have difficulty treating the handicapped person as normal in other ways. I find myself talking too loudly to my blind cousin as if his blindness affected his other senses also.

The partially or totally deaf person may feel isolated, as does the blind person. The lame person who cannot keep up with the crowd often stays home rather than to be a drag on others. Their feelings of hurt and rejection may be soundly based, for much of the time we err in two ways: we forget the handicap and expect too much, or we overemphasize the handicap and expect nothing at all. Sometimes the handicapped is treated as a nonentity and excluded from conversations and plans, which is even worse. Indifference brings a particular kind of hurt. No one likes to be ignored.

Disappointment from physical causes may include childlessness to the couple who want children. For some couples this is a tragedy, whether it is the wife's infertility or the husband's sterility. Regardless of the reason, childlessness must be faced with the same equanimity that we bring to bear on all disappointments. Babies can be adopted. If adoption is impossible or not practical, then the childless woman, like the unmarried woman, can use her time and energies in service to others' children. She can help in a kindergarten or day school, teach Sunday School, or be an advisor to girls' clubs. The husband can volunteer for work with Boy Scout troops or join the Big Brother movement or coach a church baseball team.

The terminally ill frequently are rejected even by their families. Excuses given for ignoring them vary from: "I don't feel comfortable around sickness" to "The minister calls on the sick," or "I'm too busy to visit, but Mary stays in my prayers."

I read one piteous true story of a prominent woman dying of cancer whose husband and three children stopped visiting her at the hospital because they couldn't watch her suffering. The only person faithful to the end was a girlhood friend who sat by her bedside tenderly holding her hand. The dying woman could not understand why she no longer saw her loved ones.

Many of us have tried to cheer the critically ill when old friends or close relatives no longer visited or bothered to inquire about them. It is one of the saddest hurts of all and the most undeserved because it is then we most need increased support and love. The neglectful relative who appears dutifully at Christmas bearing a poinsettia and a box of hard candy the patient can't chew merely compounds the hurt. Too many patients in nursing homes rarely or never see relatives and friends and feel deserted. This is not an opinion but verified by nurses and staff.

In observing those calling on my parents during their protracted illnesses, I drew certain conclusions, some charitable and others not. I must confess I became disillusioned by what I saw and heard in hospitals and nursing homes. There were those wonderfully faithful who came over and over, owing no duty at all. Invariably, these were dedicated Christians. One woman made Mother two afghans and refused to take money for the wool she had used. She had never met Mother before, but she attended the same church. Others should have come but stayed away and never called. This neglect is sad for the patients when they were formerly close friends or relatives.

The patient appreciates those who come often but briefly, the visitor who is never tiresome, who refrains from describing their own or others' woes, ailments, and operations, and who shows a loving concern. Nosy questions are out of order: "How much does your doctor charge?" or "Is Medicare paying for the nursing home?" or "Do you carry hospital insurance?" Even sick people have a right to privacy in personal or financial matters. For some inexplicable reason, we callers lose a sense of etiquette, decency, and tact in dealing with the sick and elderly.

If you yourself or a family member becomes ill and you belong to a church, do let the church office know. I called on a woman who had not attended the church in years even though she insisted her name remain on the rolls. In such cases, the church has to pay a per capita tax to the presbytery. When she had chatted a bit, she revealed she bore a long-standing grudge because the minister had not come to the hospital when her husband was dying.

When I asked if she had notified the office, she had not. I explained as tactfully as I could that the minister doesn't learn of such news by pure osmosis or psychic phenomenon. When I explained that the offending clergyman was long gone and hoped she would give the church another chance, she refused to budge from her belief that the church had failed her in her hour of need. Thus she had no further use for God, ministers, or the church and refused to support it with her presence or finances.

Unreasonable? Yes, but many of us are just as stubborn and petty in holding grudges against church members or our ministers for failures to minister promptly to our needs. Some of us are selfish in expecting too much personal attention when a harried minister may be scurrying from hospital to hospital, to nursing homes over a widespread area, and to members confined to their homes. What may appear as ministerial neglect to the ill or handicapped may be a lack of time to minister fully to everyone.

It is, therefore, doubly important for laypersons to assume the biblical command of calling on the sick and ministering to widows and orphans. The minister cannot do it all; nor should he be expected to.

Hurting brought on by illness or physical handicap is real, but it must be tempered with rationality and a lack of exaggerated expectations for personal attention. We may be only one of many in the church who are simultaneously suffering. We need to keep repeating to ourselves 2 Timothy 2:12: "If we suffer, we shall also reign with him: if we deny him, he also will deny us."

7

LOSS

"They shall hunger no more, neither thirst any more; neither shall the sun light on them, nor any heat. For the Lamb which is in the midst of the throne shall feed them, and shall lead them into living fountains of waters: and God shall wipe away all tears from their eyes" (Rev. 7:16-17).

Is there any reader who hasn't experienced loss of dear ones? This is a heartache we all face, and the longer we live, the more losses there will be. As a child we grieve over the death of a beloved pet or a chum moving away. In high school, a friend is killed in an auto accident or commits suicide. The latter is all too common today. We are appalled by the growing statistics of adolescent suicides.

We enter young adulthood normally experiencing little loss except from the breakup of romances. But as the years roll by, grandparents die, parents die, aunts and uncles die, brothers and sisters die, old friends die. Soon we look about us, bewildered and suddenly afraid. Here we stand alone, shivering on a barren plain with a cold wind whistling about us. We are like the last leaf of John Greenleaf Whittier's familiar poem. Where did everyone we loved disappear to? We are deserted, living in an alien world, and no longer have anyone with whom to share the past. We have only our memories to sustain us.

Within ten years' time, I lost my entire family—both parents, a favorite uncle, my younger brother, not to mention other relatives and good friends. Grandparents had died long before. Because I have no children, I now face the future alone. With the first deep-felt loss, one falters, reconnoiters, works through the grief, and then loss happens again—and again—and again.

Another loss I experienced during this same period was a house break-in when precious family heirlooms and jewelry were stolen, as well as prized objects I had brought home from travels. I consoled myself that God doesn't want us to become overly attached to material possessions, but I still feel the loss when I find myself searching for things that were stolen. Irreparable loss has been so vital a part of my life that I can write about it with profound compassion and understanding for others' pain.

When my father was last hospitalized, the doctor told me that he could not live more than a year and described in detail what would happen to his body. I had to brace myself and lean on the Psalms and the promises Christ made to sustain us through all sorrows. "For who is God save the Lord? or who is a rock save our God? It is God that guideth me with strength, and maketh my way perfect" (Ps. 18:31-32).

Similarly, five years later, the doctor warned me that Mother was near death. She survived several further crises, though, and died quietly when not expected. The twenty-third Psalm was an especial comfort through all these painful years.

Many excellent books are available on how to handle grief, for both Christians and non-Christians. They describe the five stages that grief must pass through: denial, anger, sadness and pain, guilt, and resignation. Not being a trained psychologist, I can merely say that we are told the normal person goes through these stages. However, as one who has deeply grieved and watched others coping with this hurt, I offer some practical suggestions based on sound biblical teaching.

The first and most important one is to be realistic and sensible. Christ never wants us to be foolish, impractical, or starry-eyed. He was a pragmatist Himself in all of His teaching. The parables are based on concrete practical situations and deal with common elements of daily living. His images are simple ones that everybody can understand: grass, bread, salt, light, and fire, etc. These are both elemental and symbolic. *Synecdoche* is the term that implies an object has a greater meaning than itself—such as bread standing for physical maintenance and sustenance. The point is that Christians were warned to face life clearly.

I know one woman whose husband died ten years ago. His death was a blessing that ended his long suffering. Instead of accepting its inevitability, Marsha still conspicuously parades her grief. She cannot play a hymn on the piano for Sunday School without weeping over the keyboard. She cries before her widowed friends who have had to work through their own griefs. Consequently, those who were originally sympathetic and supportive are now avoiding Marsha like the bubonic plague.

On every possible occasion, she sends sentimental, flowery memorials to the newspaper. Her friends believe, perhaps wrongly, that Marsha has had ample time to work through her grief and put it behind her. The continuous refreshment of her loss merely keeps it foremost in her mind. It is literally consuming her body and soul. This is what therapists call "abnormal grief." In Marsha's case, counsel from a minister or a good Christian psychologist would be helpful. "They that sow in tears shall reap in joy" (Ps. 126:5).

A friend widowed at the age of sixty-two had never driven a car. Even though she was fearful of busy highways, after a frustrating year of depending on others to drive her around, she decided to learn to drive. To compound her problem, she has vision in only one eye. When her ophthalmologist encouraged her to go ahead, she enrolled for lessons and finally earned her driver's license. It was the proudest day of her life. Now she is confidently driving around Indianapolis and thankful she had the courage to persist. This conquering of fear has helped her become more self-reliant.

To lessen hurt from loss of loved ones, the best remedy lies in helping to soften others' grief and putting aside one's own for the moment. Having undergone loss and received consolation, then it is one's Christian duty to help others, rather than wallowing in extended grief for years. One hears lame excuses like: "It depresses me to go to funeral homes," or "The smell of carnations sickens me," or "I prefer to remember the living." Any one of us would prefer to be elsewhere out in the sunshine enjoying ourselves. But the old-fashioned word of *duty* still applies to the Christian, although one rarely hears it in the secular world these days. All of us have duties we'd prefer to ignore if we could.

Additional pain is described by widows or widowers after the funeral. They were sustained by friends and relatives through the initial stages of grief. But, in the natural order of events, these people must return to their own lives and concerns, and then the widowed person has to face life. This is an inescapable fact for Christian and non-Christian alike. It was in this period, a recent doctor reported, that elderly widowers were most prone to commit suicide. Men have a harder time being left alone than women.

One cannot continue indefinitely to be the center of others' attention and loving sympathy. To be hurt if one is not involves being unrealistic, self-centered, and outright selfish. Life must go on, and whether we like it or not, we have to face it pretty much alone. We cannot expect even members of our own family to sacrifice a large part of their lives for us.

Too many widows become clinging vines on their grown children when they are physically well and perfectly capable of standing on their own feet. They will have to make an enlarged circle of friends, for the widow is often excluded from affairs that cater to couples. The widower may be more fortunate here, for an extra man is always in demand, although some grieving widowers reject invitations. Social exclusion may hurt for a while, but one must face reality. The newly alone must look for new friends among other widows and widowers, divorcees, and singles. Again, false pride may keep one from taking this step.

A dear friend Sarah lost her beloved husband after his long battle against cancer. In my estimation, Sarah has been a model widow. Immediately, she cleared out her husband's clothes and belongings, refusing to succumb to clinging to objects. At the church she took on new tasks and made herself available to counsel with other new widows. One day a week she volunteered in community service. Within the year she joined a tour to Europe, perhaps beyond the financial capacity of some widows, but one she could well afford. She enrolled in an adult class at a nearby university.

Sarah mentions Harry casually, but there are no long stories about his marvelous attributes or her more grievous loss than other persons'. Sarah is blessed with a loving daughter and three delightful grandchildren for whom she occasionally baby-sits, but she does not dominate her daughter's life or family or unduly impose on their time.

Sarah's adjustment to living alone has been admirable and a model for other women. She had long been ready, a dedicated Christian well grounded in biblical principles. When the inevitable came and Harry died, she applied what she had always professed. She is attractive and may remarry, but she makes no fetish of being on a frantic hunt for a second husband. "Weeping may endure for a night, but joy cometh in the morning" (Ps. 30:5).

On the other hand, if the reader is interested in remarrying, experts tell us not to be too shy to let friends know you'd like to meet suitable prospects. Many older widows and widowers grew up in the days when proper ladies waited breathlessly for gallant knights to search them out. Many older men have forgotten how to pursue a woman and capture her interest or even how to ask for a date.

Both men and women can be timid about expressing any normal interest in the opposite sex. On the other side of the coin, I'm not urging outright aggressiveness, as happened to a relative. When he was left a widower, women descended upon him like a flock of harpies. Eager matchmakers in his church thrust telephone numbers in his hand to call women he had not even met. He was inundated with casseroles and invitations to dinner. To him, this feminine onslaught was a joke, for he was perfectly capable of seeking out his own companionship. This kind of brazen conduct can become embarrassing to a man and makes lone women look ridiculous in men's eyes. Overaggressiveness still tends to frighten men away even in these liberated times rather than attracting them. They still prefer to be the pursuer, according to my men friends, and a touch of mystery and reserve in a woman is attractive to them.

Even the ladylike woman, however, can whisper in a close friend's ear that she is ready to meet men and to go out socially. This usually occurs after a suitable period of mourning. Too abrupt a return to the social whirl can still cause raised eyebrows and whispers. She doesn't need to consider each one as a marriage prospect but, initially, only as a companion and escort. Just because she eats a meal with a man doesn't need to imply that intimacy will follow. It's amazing what a new man's interest can do for a woman overcoming hurt from loss. Just having a reason to dress up in her best is a spur to her spirits. This same rule applies to men. A man is usually more shy and more loath to express a desire to meet women, but many relationships have developed from a friend inviting a widower to dinner to meet a mutual friend.

One widow in middle age was jolly and outgoing, although not expecially pretty. Her friends joked that anywhere they went, there was Mrs. Gadabout in evidence. She belonged to every club in town. It wasn't long until Mrs. Gadabout met a gadabout widower, a stocky, cheerful man. Their second marriage was a resounding success. Their secret was apparently to make themselves available to new experiences, responsive to overtures, and not too rigid in hopes and expectations. Too much timidity can be a detriment, and for persons experiencing hurt after loss, it can prove a disaster. We need to push ourselves at times, be willing to take chances and to form new relationships, even with risk involved.

However, a hurting person can fall easy prey to fraudulent schemes and outright scoundrels of both sexes. We are particularly vulnerable when we are blue and lonely and looking for any companionship. We should make ourselves available, but we must not be gullible. How many lonely women have promptly signed over money and property to charming rascals and have been hurt a second time entirely through their own foolishness? How many gullible men have been taken in by scheming younger women who flatter their ego? "There's no fool like an old fool" is folk wisdom.

It is wise to check up a bit on any suitor before succumbing to blandishments, especially in a whirlwind courtship. Your banker can find out if he has a bank account anywhere or has a reliable reputation. Don't be too proud to do a little checking before making foolish decisions. It is certainly unwise to hand over money blindly to anyone on brief acquaintance or to sign papers without a reputable lawyer's advice.

Personally, I believe a single person is indiscreet to advertise in lovelorn or personal columns. Some readers may disagree. By doing so, both women and men have been taken advantage of, or at the worst, many have met ill fates. To be so blatant about one's solitude is an open invitation to be cheated and deceived.

Some people are so desperately lonely they will do anything short of murder to find companionship. An elderly friend let a charming young woman move into her house with the understanding she would help with housework and cooking. After a while, the widow's son became suspicious of the arrangement, for the guest was putting pressure on the homeowner to sign over her funds and home to a notorious cult. The son ordered the young woman out of the house, leaving his mother confused and uncertain of what had happened. She had liked the young woman and had not suspected she was being taken advantage of. This ploy is a favorite one of those preying on the elderly.

One can meet decent men and woman with comparable interests and values in volunteer work, churches, craft classes, political meetings, university classes, or other such legitimate places. It is wise to avoid becoming intimate too hastily and on too little acquaintance.

The hurting, lonely person who has suffered a loss needs

to be careful. God watches over us because his eye is on the sparrow, but He expects us also to use the common sense He has not granted to the sparrow.

I told the story earlier of Fanny who had not adjusted to the loss of her model eighty-six-year-old husband Carl. Her story demonstrates the need to prepare ourselves well in advance to bear the loss of loved ones. We cannot close our eyes to the reality of the deaths of those we love. For lose them we shall, at least in this life.

Those of us who lived through World War II or any of the succeeding wars can recall vividly what it meant when those ominous telegrams arrived reporting deaths in battle. My father coached a baseball team of fine young men before the war. Of the nine first stringers, three were killed in battle in World War II. Dad wept over each one as if he had lost a son. What a tragic loss! Yet parents had the consolation that their sons gave their lives for their country and died honorably. Many young women have lost fiancés in war. England never recovered from her monumental losses of her finest youth in both world wars.

My brother, a Marine of the famed Fifth Division, served on Guam, Tinian, Iwo Jima, and Saipan, four of the fiercest campaigns in the South Pacific. He went in ahead of the lines and laid telephone wires. What pain and anxiety it was for my parents each time news was reported of the Fifth Marines' landing on another Japanese-help island and their resistance. My brother miraculously returned from his service but was one of the few in his outfit who did. What heartache for him to witness his buddies killed before his eyes! Does a man or woman ever recover from the horrors of war? A body may survive, but what of the soul and spirit? Only God can heal such sorrows. "I will not leave you comfortless: I will come to you" (John 14:18).

Like many of you, I have lost a spouse through divorce after twenty-two years of marriage. Psychologists tell us that divorce may be harder to bear than widowhood because one is not surrounded by the love and sympathy of others as the widowed are. Also one is faced with a sense of failure and the loss of what was once a promising love. I met different reactions even though I was adjudged the "innocent party." Concern and aid came from my ever-faithful parents; sympathy came from a few old friends I notified of my change of address; and indifference came from others as though I had contracted a communicable disease and needed to be quarantined. The latter attitude hurts when it is from people whom one loves. The only solution is to ignore the rejections and be thankful that someone has stood by through the ordeal.

In this respect, I was more fortunate than others. Some friends who have undergone a painful divorce have had no one else to rely on. Divorced persons of both sexes tell the same tales of rejection and harsh isolation when they most need consolation and understanding. In any set of circumstances and for whatever causes, divorce is one of the most hurtful loss situations one can undergo.

Through observation, and listening to others tell their experiences, I have concluded that the persons who best overcome hurt from any type of loss are those who become involved in life and lay aside their grief as quickly as possible. They develop new interests and continue those they already had. They face life realistically and without excessive self-pity, self-condemnation, or self-centeredness. For a committed Christian, it is a lack of faith to grieve excessively for one who is now with the Lord. Of course, we miss those loved ones; we must work through the stages of grief. We shall never forget them, but we remind ourselves that they live now in paradise in God's presence. If they were not Christians, then we can only trust in God's mercy and compassion when our loved ones stand before Him for judgment.

A good verse to remember in seeking companions after loss is Matthew 10:16: "Behold, I send you forth as sheep in the midst of wolves: be ye therefore wise as serpents, and harmless as doves."

8
Gossip

"Love your enemies, bless them that curse you, do good to them that hate you, and pray for them which despitefully use you, and persecute you" (Matt. 5:44).

An amusing experience happened to me, one that happens to many teachers. A student asked, "Are you and Mr. Halvorsen going together?"

"Of course not," I replied, surprised. "Whatever gave you that idea?"

"Well, he's always in your room talking, so I thought he must be your boyfriend. All the kids think so."

"Mr. Halvorsen and I are discussing students," I said and smiled to myself, for I was at least fifteen years older than he. He was a counselor who often came to my room and sat by my desk to discuss a mutual problem with a student.

Teachers, ministers, doctors—those in the social services —are prone to hurt from gossip. Students are forever looking for romances between teachers and see one in every friendly exchange. I must admit that my friends and I were the same way in high school. We were dying for Mr. Falkland, a handsome widower with a young daughter, to marry Miss Carter, a young, pretty teacher whom we adored. After dating Miss Carter a while and escorting her to school dances, Mr. Falkland disappointed us by marrying an older woman he had known in his youth. What Miss Carter's reaction was, we didn't know, but we students thought she looked sad for a while. We couldn't understand why he had passed over such a prize.

Later Miss Carter herself became the subject of an ugly, whispering campaign involving her and a married administrator. I was out of high school by that time, but I never believed the stories about my girlhood idol. Even though the disgruntled student who originated the salacious tale later confessed he had lied about what he supposedly saw, the irrevocable damage had been wreaked in the community. Two fine reputations had been permanently scarred. Not long thereafter the administrator left the school system and moved out of state.

Miss Carter remained until her retirement, but I often wondered how she had the courage to continue. As far as I know, she never married. Unbelievably, I still hear that nasty gossip dredged up these many years later. "Thou shalt not bear false witness against thy neighbor" is one of the Ten Commandments (Ex. 20:16).

Tragic hurt is caused by wagging, evil tongues. And how can one respond to malicious gossip? Some of the worst is heard among supposedly dedicated church members who cannot resist circulating a juicy story.

My former father-in-law was a minister and a wise one. If he were called into an unsavory neighborhood, he took his wife with him. If he visited a laywoman at night in an emergency, his wife went along even if she waited in the car at the curb. He was careful never to give the slightest appearance of evil, and thus died a man about whom there was never a hint of scandal.

Hearts have been shattered and illness or even suicide provoked by vicious tongues. Probably no one is totally immune from gossip because we do not live like unsullied plaster saints. Perfectly innocent actions are often misunderstood by the best of us, and we may misinterpret what we think we see. That is why it is wise to be discreet about what tales we pass along indiscriminately. Shakespeare's play *Othello* is a tragic statement of what a wicked tongue can do to a man's spirit.

Hurt from gossip can result from our own actions that we know were wrong or unwise. We later regret our indiscretions and pray for forgiveness. Few of us have escaped doing things that we regretted or were ashamed of in retrospect. If we haven't, then we are either unearthly angels, flapping our wings, or we are closing our eyes to our sins and excusing our weaknesses and failures.

How should one react to a friend who is hurting because of gossip? If the talk is true, should one drop the friend who has erred? We all hesitate to be busybodies or to invade another's inner sanctum. It seems the logical action for a Christian is to talk lovingly with the friend, explaining frankly that certain actions have caused talk. If the offender wishes to avoid further gossip, one should refrain from whatever the error is. That is the responsibility of a true friend.

It is vitally important, though, not to sound judgmental or self-righteous if we want to help the friend. Our human tendency is to be judgmental if we cannot approve of another's actions even though we are fond of the person. The Pharisees in their self-righteousness and strict adherence to the letter of the law greatly angered Jesus, and He reserved His harshest criticisms for their hypocrisy. Many Christians frighten hurting people away from the church by their holier-than-thou attitudes. They tend to forget that sin is sin, and we are all sinners in God's sight to one degree or another.

We like to think that others' sins are greater than ours. We are especially intolerant of sins of the flesh or of sins we ourselves do not commit. Psychologists warn us that we criticize others for tendencies we see within ourselves. The man who may condemn his brother for gambling may be a tightfisted employer who underpays and bullies his employees. Sins of the spirit must concern us also. A loving spirit is always most helpful to others rather than one of negative criticism. Hardly anyone responds to that.

Subsequently, we must lay the matter in God's hands and pray for the friends being gossiped about. We have done all we can. We have also let our friends know we stand beside them, even though we do not entirely approve of their actions.

If the gossip is based on spite, rumor, or jealousy, then it is our duty to scotch it wherever we can. The old adage is "Silence is golden," but as my pastor often says, it is plain yellow. If we don't defend a friend when we know the gossip is unjustified or exaggerated, we are as guilty as the critics. We don't want to "make waves," so we sit back, keep our lips closed, and let the talk eddy around us, too cowardly to get involved. "Let your speech be alway with grace, seasoned with salt, that ye may know how ye ought to answer every man" (Col. 4:6).

Gossip can permanently ruin reputations as well as bring great hurt. The more sensitive and idealistic the person, the more one is hurt by slander. This is as true of men as of women. One who doesn't care what he does is amoral, or one who is hardened and cynical rarely worries about what is said about him. He does as he pleases and lets the devil take the hindmost. The man or woman who has a sense of decency and honor values their reputation.

One of my mother's favorite admonitions was for us children to act honorably and to be known as having integrity. Any unwarranted gossip is a blot on that integrity.

How to handle gossip for both the listener and the subject of it is found in the biblical injunction that only God knows the heart. We need only to please Him, to answer to Him, and not to placate those around us. This is extremely hard to practice, though, for as Christians, we wish to be well thought of and to be admired. We are told to let our light shine and to be the salt of the earth.

The proven best defense against gossip is to cling to one's dignity and to reject the overpowering temptation to justify, explain, or argue. If the gossip is based on only rumor, it will eventually evaporate into mist. If there is ample ground for the gossip, we can't expect to brazen it out. We have to eliminate the cause at once, repent, and ask forgiveness for the sin, whatever it is. No other route is open to a Christian.

To sum up, I am convinced that a dignified, unflappable stance can do wonders in this situation. We witness far too little dignity, modesty, and reserve in today's world. The current tendency is to tell all, to "let it all hang out," to broadcast our intimate secrets, and to be unashamed of nothing or unshocked by an indiscretion.

The person who faces gossip with dignity will eventually win admiration from even hostile quarters. Princess Alexandra of England acted with dignity when her husband, then Prince of Wales and later Edward VII, was a notorious womanizer who publicly flaunted his affairs. The princess was gracious enough to remain silent and even to receive at least one of his mistresses at court. During those episodes that must have been humiliating to a woman of exalted position and renowned beauty, Alexandra never lost her quiet composure.

Mrs. Lyndon Johnson has conducted herself with poise through the unflattering, posthumous revelations of her husband's peccadilloes with other women. The present, popular mayor of Indianapolis, William Hudnut, an ordained Presbyterian minister, maintained his dignity and honor by making no public statements of justification during his divorce.

"Who art thou that judgest another man's servant? to his own master he standeth or falleth. Yes, he shall be holden up: for God is able to make him stand" (Rom. 14:4).

9
Failure

"They that wait upon the Lord shall renew their strength; they shall mount up with wings as eagles; they shall run, and not be weary; and they shall walk, and not faint" (Isa. 40:31).

Who of us has not failed at something? We read the biographies of Abraham Lincoln, Harry Truman, and Sinclair Lewis, among others, and find that all met failure after failure. The humiliations the latter faced because of his ugliness and midwestern background when he went East to college helped create the novelist who won the Nobel Prize for Literature. Ninety percent of writers have endured countless rejections before their work has been deemed publishable. To his friend and biographer A. E. Hotchner, even a master like Ernest Hemingway admitted crying over cold rejections early in his career.

Few of us reach adulthood without meeting failures of one kind or another. Psychologists term these minor deaths. These failures come for various reasons. We attempt mastery where we possess no talent. We unrealistically exaggerate our abilities. We may not use abilities correctly that we do have. School conferences abound with disappointed parents who expect too much from the child.

As I am writing this book, a letter to an advice columnist reports that a child receiving C's on his report card was grounded for six weeks. His parents expected him to earn A's and B's as his siblings did. My heart ached for that child. Having taught as many as five children from the same family, I found them all different. Wise parents don't expect their children to be identical or to earn the same grades; nor do they make unflattering comparisons.

The only reason to punish a child for earning C's, a respectable grade, is if the child is not trying or has unusually high abilities. Some parents are too proud to admit that they have average children. They push them beyond their capabilities, a rejection hard for a child to handle.

One may become gripped by the very fear of failure itself in everything he undertakes. Whatever the cause, the ensuing hurt can permanently damage his self-esteem. Some children never recover from early failures and label themselves failures throughout life. Like lemmings rushing blindly toward the sea, they seek out failure and stoically prepare themselves ahead to meet it. All readers probably know persons like this, determined that defeat will come no matter how they try to avoid it.

We have to remind ourselves until it sinks into our consciousness that as long as we try, we are never failures in God's eyes. Only those who give up are personal failures. A passage that can sustain us through failure is Philippians 3:13, "This one thing I do, forgetting those things which are behind, and reaching forth unto those things which are before."

At times, failure is brought on by unforeseen circumstances such as the bank closings and stock market crash in the Great Depression. Those of us old enough to remember those times or to have heard parents describe them know that many families' life savings were lost. Neighbors on our street lost their homes because of inability to pay on their mortgages. Men who could not withstand the shock of being wiped out jumped from windows. Other stronger men, like my father, squared their shoulders and took any work they could find to keep body and soul together. My mother went to work to help meet expenses. They struggled through these hard times together, and we were never in want. Today there are government bulwarks against total financial failure such as unemployment compensation, welfare, food stamps, and even reduced mortgage rates for those with low incomes.

In spite of these valuable supports, there appears today a general lack of moral stamina and grit to understand the least failure or disappointment. Many people buckle under at the first hint of stress and give up. Psychiatrists' waiting rooms are packed with those unfortunates who have never "found" themselves, whatever that means. I heard a middle school counselor announce in a meeting that young children must be protected from any kind of failure. Is it any wonder that some of them, when older, crack at the first sign of black clouds on the horizon? They have never been taught or prepared to face disappointment.

It is our mental attitude that can make or break us when hurt from failure comes. It can spur us on to do better, or it can defeat us. We become frozen, stymied, if we concentrate on previous failures, afraid to try the new and challenging. Rudyard Kipling's poem "If" was one we memorized in school. It was an ideal held up to us.

As we look back over our lives, we will concede that our failures and successes seem to balance out. But aren't you proud that you tried again and again? That despite your disappointments and hurts, you became a tough survivor in the game of life? And didn't you learn something positive from those failures? Why you needed to work on an annoying habit or a defeating flaw in your personality? Where your real talents lay? When you needed to strike out of a hopeless, no-win situation?

It may be a cliché, but it is also true that we learn more through our failures than through our successes if we let ourselves. We blithely accept the successes uncritically as our due and do not examine ourselves as we do when we fail. Then we want to know where we went astray and why.

The major lesson I learned from my own failures was to be more sympathetic and understanding and not to expect miracles from myself or others. As a young teacher I was critical of small errors, proud and impatient with those I considered less intelligent than I. Every situation was either black or white, with no margin for human fallibility. I saw little excuse for the foolish mistakes that others made. In my youthful eyes, only the stupid, inept, lazy, or careless failed.

But the Lord shook His mighty head, took me firmly in hand, and worked on that haughty, critical spirit. He let me suffer some dismal failures of my own until He had molded me into a more malleable state, so He could teach me some lessons in humility. I was one of His own, and the Lord disciplines us in love as parents do their naughty children. "For whom the Lord loveth he chasteneth, and scourgeth every son whom he receiveth" (Heb. 12:6).

Late in my career a student told me with a sly twinkle that I had certainly mellowed since I had taught his mother before him. I laughed, but it was all too true. Those abject failures had made me a much better teacher, more compassionate toward struggling students. I still challenged them to do their best, but I no longer expected what they could not accomplish. I learned to value the students who did their best and plugged on conscientiously even if their work were only *D* quality.

After I had taught a while, I enrolled in a graduate course in which I sat utterly bewildered, unable to understand what was going on. The professor's philosophy and interpretations of the literature, secular and humanistic in nature, were foreign to me. Nor could I understand what she expected in the weekly papers she assigned. I wrote three successive papers that were marked "unsatisfactory." There was no comment as to what made it so. She held each paper until after another one was due, so there was no chance to learn from previous errors. As a teacher who wrote copious comments on my students' papers, I couldn't understand her methods.

I simply couldn't believe I was failing. Why, I'd always earned *A*'s on my writing. Hadn't I been valedictorian of my class? Quite embarrassed but determined to better my standing, I requested a conference with this professor. I can still picture her raised eyebrows, superior manner, cool eyes, and pursed lips. She couldn't seem to understand why I was so obtuse and thickheaded. I sat humbled by her desk, just as students had shrunk in their chairs beside mine, while I must have impressed them in the same way. What a lesson in humility that was!

Finally, I did produce a paper that earned a "satisfactory" from this dread martinet. It was as though I had conquered Mount Everest! I completed the course with a *B* grade, which I appreciated under the circumstances. That course was the low point of my academic career. Yet I recognize that it was more valuable to me than the ones in which I excelled, for afterward, I could empathize with how my students felt lost in a class.

God humbles us in His inimitable way when we become proud and cocky about our abilities. Because He loves us, He schools us in the exclusive college of hard knocks reserved for His own. We know that some of our failures are for discipline. At the time we agonize and complain, but in retrospect, we understand what He was doing. We sheep know the voice of our Shepherd. If we are wise, we will come when He summons and follow where He leads us into the right pasture and through the narrow gate. "When he putteth forth his own sheep, he goeth before them, and the sheep follow him: for they know his voice" (John 10:4).

Pride does go before a fall. We can see many instances of it when we are perceptive. A young friend was visibly proud of her successful marriage, handsome husband, and tastefully decorated home. In popular parlance, she "had it all." They were an engaging couple who apparently shared many interests and led an exciting, worldly life.

Bettina was intelligent and poised but as intolerant of others' lesser assets as I had once been. She had never failed at anything in her life, and she proudly let everyone know it. Her life had been a succession of getting just what she wanted. Bettina and her husband were nominal Christians who didn't let the church interfere with their pursuit of pleasure. They did not want children to clutter up their lives, either.

After eight years of marriage, Bettina's husband suddenly deserted her for another woman. She claimed she hadn't once suspected anything was missing in their relationship. Of all the women I have known who have had this happen, Bettina reacted the most drastically. She went to pieces, as the saying goes, and had to be committed to a psychiatric ward. It took her several months to recover her equilibrium. The abrupt loss of her husband had been such a blow to her pride that it almost destroyed her.

Bettina left her job she had professed to love, began working toward a graduate degree, gave that up after a few months, returned to the psychiatric ward, and from there entered a business career. The last I heard of her, she had remarried and apparently regained her stability, but it took her a long while.

God does have a way of bringing us to our knees or even throwing us flat on our faces when we least expect it. Whether or not He causes the crisis, He seems to stand aloof and allows us to suffer it. It can be a most humbling experience and can change our lives and our complete outlook. My divorced friend lost her arrogance and pride, and her demeanor became more subdued and gentle. I believe she became a finer woman after the divorce than before it. This is not to imply that a painful divorce is ever a panacea, but through hers, Bettina developed a more loving character.

God can lift us above and beyond any kind of failure, no matter where it lies. He doesn't expect us to wallow in the mire of self-pity or to cease trying to pull ourselves out of it. "For God hath not given us the spirit of fear; but of power, and of love, and of a sound mind" (2 Tim. 1:7).

If we don't love anyone or let ourselves get involved in living, we never will be hurt. We can shut ourselves in our houses, lock our doors, pull the blinds, cut ourselves off from others, take no risks, make no commitments, and lead a comfortable, failure-proof life. But what fun is that? What challenge? What excitement? The exhilaration of living comes from taking chances, daring to love, meeting new adventures, risking failure again and again, pulling ourselves up, dusting ourselves off, and trudging on, ready for the next challenge.

It is in the area of love relationships that we most often encounter hurt. Failure there leaves us wondering if we are totally unlovable or worthy of love, even though we use all those fabulous products advertised to make us desirable. God answers that haunting question clearly for us. He loves us unstintingly, so we *are* worthy. If another person fails to return our love or stops loving us, that does not necessarily mean we are unworthy. Love must be given voluntarily and freely. We cannot earn it, command it, buy it, or demand it.

If we are honest with ourselves—and we must be if we wish to master hurt and disappointment—we should recognize that love relationships are always risks. We lay ourselves wide open to another person's whims when we fall in love and thus become eminently vulnerable. Even if the love ends, we have memories of the good times. If bad times predominated and ended in disillusionment, the relationship was not worth continuing, and we have to write it off to experience.

If we continue choosing the wrong love partners who invariably fail or disappoint us, we undoubtedly need professional counseling to see why we consistently make poor choices. Why do we let ourselves be taken advantage of and deceived? We may be individuals, either male or female, who love unwisely and never gain any satisfaction from a relationship, but only pain.

All aspects of life are temporary, and we have to accept that a passionate love may not last. It often flames up and burns out quickly, leaving only a gray residue of dull ashes. Some loves do endure until death, but all do not. We may fall in love and fail, as we do in other aspects of our lives, without being failures as total persons.

Hurting over lost love is especially poignant because, if we are romanticists, we prefer to believe the idealistic love songs and poems that romantic love never fails. But adults change in their values, tastes, and ideas. No one who is normal remains static. What attracts one at eighteen will not at thirty and certainly not at fifty. We entrust our hearts and souls to someone, believing that person is the only one for us. Then if the love wanes and flickers out, we are left hurting, sure that we shall never, never love again. It isn't worth the pain.

But God can heal even this type of hurt, for He can do all things. "And Jesus came and spake unto them, saying, All power is given unto me in heaven and in earth" (Matt. 28:18). We should never limit His capabilities and resources. In due time, we meet someone else, our eyes lock, our pulses begin to throb, and another romantic attachment begins. And contrary to the beliefs of the young, this thrilling event can happen at any age. I recently read of an eighty-three-year-old widow who remarried.

This type of hurt can be avoided by never letting oneself love, but human love is one of the richest joys of life. Normal persons long to experience its excitement at least once.

Too often, though, in erotic love, we neglect to apply our biblical and spiritual principles. We tend to separate them completely from what the Bible teaches, yet many beautiful passages in the Old Testament have to do with the love between men and women. "The Song of Solomon" is exquisite poetry, one of the loveliest celebrations of love ever written.

We tend to separate erotic (sexual) love from *philia* (brotherly) love or *agape* (God's love) and treat them differently, but they all stem from the same source: God. The Bible speaks clearly to hurt from failure of erotic love.

Perhaps that man or woman who summarily rejected you was never right for you in God's eyes. Keep reminding yourself that He has a predetermined purpose for your life. Doubtless the erstwhile lover did not fit into that purpose, and God interceded for your welfare. This reassurance to yourself can assuage the pain of a broken romance when nothing else suffices.

"The fruit of the Spirit is love, joy, peace, longsuffering, gentleness, goodness, faith" (Gal. 5:22).

10

Appearance

"Favour is deceitful, and beauty is vain; but a woman that feareth the Lord, she shall be praised" (Prov. 31:30).

Models and ideas of beauty and masculinity have existed since the beginning of history. From Helen of Troy to Cleopatra to Madame Pompadour to Lily Langtry to Marilyn Monroe, beautiful women have been admired by both sexes. Men who have been symbols to women include David of the Old Testament; Charles II of England; Charles Dickens; James O'Neill, actor-father of Eugene; John F. Kennedy; and Clark Gable.

How wonderful to be so beautiful that our face alone would launch a thousand ships! To have men falling at our feet and losing empires out of mad desire! Or to be such an appealing man that women haunt our doors for just a brief glance and a nod.

Today men drool over centerfold pictures of gorgeous women, causing their wives to indignantly bar such magazines from the house. Women leaf through glamorous fashion magazines and envy the trim figures of the bored-looking models. Men study sports and health magazines, hoping to resemble the masculine models there. Then we look with dismay at our own imperfect bodies and faces and wonder why we had to be shortchanged and created so ordinary looking.

Ecclesiastes 1:2 warns us: "Vanity of vanities, saith the Preacher, vanity of vanities; all is vanity." But we disregard that admonition. All of us, either male or female, possess at least a modicum of vanity about our looks and yearn to be attractive.

Researchers report the astounding fact that more money is spent annually on cosmetics than that given to churches or spent on schools combined in the United States. At Christmas time in 1985 the television news announced that three billion dollars a year was spent on perfume alone. Women flit from fashion to fashion: one season in the miniskirt, the next in the maxi-skirt. We switch from the formfitting coat to the enveloping cape. We laugh at ourselves, but we slavishly continue to follow the fads and style dictates from Paris, New York, and Los Angeles.

Men adopt fashions more discreetly; nevertheless, they follow fashion dictates in business and professional garb. The gray flannel suit became the symbol of success.

With this exaggerated emphasis on exterior attractiveness, disappointment can result from lack of good looks, imagined homeliness, or out-and-out deformity. We painfully measure ourselves against flawless beauties and handsome heroes on television. We view with disdain our own marred and imperfect bodies, forgetting that superb photographers with expensive cameras can lessen or brush out imperfections. We blindly discount the fact that only one woman out of a possible ten thousand is a true beauty or one man an Adonis.

What woman does not contemplate her thick legs, bulging hips, or sagging bust and yearn to look as she did at eighteen? What man does not hate his balding head, his oversize stomach, and drooping shoulders and envy the Hollywood he-man? And oddly enough, no matter how lovely a woman is, she emphasizes her one poor feature over the good ones. If you doubt that, read the testimonies of our current reigning beauties about how some trivial imperfection bothers them. And men refuse to believe that it is their character and tenderness that attract women and hold them, not necessarily their appearance.

Some of the world's best husbands are men who would not attract a second glance. But the matter of appearance is more crucial to women than to men. Most men can put aside such matters more easily than women, for our culture equates worth in women with their outer appearance.

What constitutes our idea of attractiveness also differs. We have all heard that beauty is in the eye of the beholder. Eras have different standards. The lush beauties of Rubens are not the same as the glowing ones of Titian. Our society puts a premium on slim, rangy figures. In men the tall, brawny masculine type appeals or the small, boyish types that appeal to the maternal instinct in women.

One of the loveliest, most memorable women I ever knew was a teacher in my high school. Her modest wardrobe was limited to a few changes because teachers were poorly paid in those times. She wore few cosmetics, and her hair was drawn back from her oval face in a plain fashion. Her figure could not be called seductive by the furtherest stretch of the imagination. She spoke in a sweet, gentle manner. I never heard her raise her voice or say a mean thing, and I knew her for forty years. The beauty of her character and her spirituality cast a radiant aura about her. I can picture her at her desk as vividly as if she were before me. What an impact she made upon us students! We girls aspired to be like her. I considered her a true beauty, yet by today's artificial, plastic standards she would be passed over. Her beautiful spirit arose from a lifelong Christian commitment.

The photographs of novelist Edna Ferber reveal her as a short woman with a massive head on a tiny frame and plain facial features except for large, expressive eyes. Although she never married, Miss Ferber had several marriage proposals. With her sparkling wit and agile intellect, she held her own among the famed, sophisticated circle at the Algonquin Round Table in New York City.

Other famous women would never have won beauty contests in either their days or ours. Yet they were greatly admired by contemporaries as attractive, charming women. Among these could be included Martha Washington; Wallis Warfield, later Duchess of Windsor; Florence Nightingale; Bess Truman; Helen Hayes; Mamie Eisenhower; and Barbra

Streisand. Many women and especially teenage girls suffer unjustified heartache over real or imagined lack of outer physical beauty. Some of this hurt is involved in teenagers starving themselves into anorexia.

Haven't you known women who had not an outstanding feature, yet when they entered a room, everyone noticed? There was a zest, an enthusiasm, an erect carriage, a sparkle in the eyes, or a dynamic personality irresistible to both sexes. In addition, a Christian woman radiates a calmness of spirit, an inner poise, and an air of self-worth because she knows she is precious in God's sight. All these qualities make her attractive far more than mere superficial prettiness can. True beauty is internal as well as external.

Without false modesty and disparagement of her natural assets, she makes the most of her looks. She dresses becomingly and stylishly, but not faddishly or extravagantly. She keeps her hair styled in modern fashion. If she wishes, she uses cosmetics tastefully. Yet none of these embellishments are predominant in her life; nor does she make a full-time fetish of her looks. They merely enhance the lovely, inner spirit, the most important asset of all.

The woman who refuses to accept her own appearance and age appears doubtful of her self-worth. Is there any sight more pathetic than the old woman stumbling along on spike heels, in a knee-length, tight skirt, and wearing garish makeup? Women are embarrassed for her because in her attempt to look young and attractive, she merely succeeds in looking absurd.

In America the overemphasis on youth convinces women middle-aged or past that they have nothing left to offer. They lose the very charm and glow and spirit that once attracted others. Conversely, European men often admire and consider more interesting the woman past the first flush of youth. True loveliness and charm have little to do with one's physical age.

The excessively vain woman who refuses to wear much-needed glasses or headgear in inclement weather is emphasizing false values. What worthwhile person judges another on such foolish minutiae? When we think others are that attentive to our looks, we show a self-centeredness unsuitable to a Christian woman. "Favour is deceitful, and beauty is vain: but a woman that feareth the Lord, she shall be praised" (Prov. 31:30).

Being an incurable romantic and inveterate matchmaker, I watched after a plain, dowdy colleague was widowed. Competing with her for masculine attention in the high school were three single women judged "knockouts" by the male faculty. And who was the first one of these four unmarried women to win a good husband? Of course, the plain, quiet widow.

As a keen observer of human nature, I analyzed the reason as I saw it. She was slightly older than the others, not nearly so dazzling and stylish, but modest, sweet, soft-spoken, and evidently she had learned what appealed to a man better than they. Of the three striking beauties, two have not married, and the third has been married and divorced twice.

Hurting and disappointment should not result from superficialities. They should be reserved for life's real tragedies. If hurting does come from shallow thinking, then we have our priorities in poor alignment. Old Testament injunctions about style, such as women not cutting their hair, do not apply today in most denominations. We need to keep our eyes fixed on worthwhile criteria.

Pain can come from other causes recounted in this book, but, generally, unless we are disfigured badly—and modern plastic surgery can remedy even that—we should keep our eyes on the Lord, not ourselves. He will use us in spite of our physical imperfections.

Oddly enough, in the final analysis, we don't know what about us attracts others. It may be a quality that we are unaware of. In this wicked world with its constantly shifting values and lack of moral absolutes, sterling character is still more important and desirable than a glittering personality and outer good looks.

"For wisdom is better than rubies; and all the things that may be desired are not to be compared to it" (Prov. 8:11).

11

Displacement

"My presence shall go with thee, and I will give thee rest" (Ex. 33:14).

A traumatic experience for many persons is being forced to relinquish their homes and possessions. This can occur because of physical inability to keep up property any longer, financial setbacks, or in divorce, losing the house to a spouse. Recently, I read of one widely publicized case in which a husband bulldozed down the house where his ex-wife and small children lived. Other men applauded his act.

Whatever the cause, one feels a tug at the heartstrings to pull up roots and move from a beloved dwelling or community or separate oneself from one's old friends.

My widowed mother sold her home when her health and eyesight failed and moved into my home. We both dreaded the day her household belongings were auctioned off. Wisely, she remained away, but I had to be present to protect her interests. She brought with her her china, sterling silver, and a few other prized items. She had given away to friends and relatives other items, but many of her best loved possessions were sold at auction. She and Dad had worked hard to acquire nice things, and both had taken pride in their home.

For months Mother would ask wistfully, "What happened to the pineapple upside-down cake pan?" or "Did my grinder go out in the auction?" Auctions also hurt because one gets very little for most long-used items.

Many of us have lived through this upsetting situation either for ourselves or relatives or may face it one day. Relinquishing the accumulations of a lifetime can be a shock almost as strong as losing a person. One has lost a vital part of oneself. I shed tears that day I watched my parents' former household on the auction block. I was watching the end of an era and the loss of memories. Nowadays, yard and garage sales proliferate.

One moves from a house into an apartment, crowding into a small area when one has been used to ample space. Or it may be a single room in a retirement home or nursing home. In Mother's case, she moved from a home with a large yard to a bedroom in my home, then to a tiny room in a nursing home, shared with another patient. These successive steps can break the spirit of the strongest man or woman. Walls are slowly closing in, and death is crouching in wait around the corner. We become acutely conscious of those precious remaining days to share together.

There is the displacement of leaving a community where one has longtime friends, church, and neighbors. Perhaps a new super highway is coming through, and the land is requisitioned by the state. A son or daughter begs the aging parents or widowed mother or father to move nearby. The upsetting change may be accomplished; then the son is transferred to another state. The displaced parents are left high and dry, vainly wishing they had stayed where they were. Acts 17:28 says, "In him we live, and move, and have our being"; wherever we are, we know the Lord is with us.

Making repeated adjustments and new friends in old age is not easy even for an extroverted person. I was amazed, though, that my bedridden mother made new friends to the end of her life. Her outgoing nature and keen humor attracted people. She always had a little joke to pass on to the nurses and aides. After her death I still receive calls from people who miss her cheerful presence. Mother had that prized art of being a good listener and conversationalist, even when she was in constant pain. This precious asset wins friends everywhere. "A merry heart maketh a cheerful countenance: but by sorrow of the heart the spirit is broken" (Prov. 15:13).

Another type of displacement is suffered increasingly by younger women deserted by their husbands. They may be awarded child support, but their own incomes are cut, alimony rarely being granted today, and they are forced to find less expensive quarters. In some cases the husband avoids the court-ordered, support payments, so the mother is forced to apply to welfare for aid. More and more women are finding themselves in this precarious situation. Displacement follows, plus the anxiety of coping with the problems of a single parent. Even men are being faced with these problems, for they are being awarded the custody of children. This makes for a whole change in life-style of the single male parent.

Also, parents are being confronted with adult children moving back home just when the parents were feeling free of responsibility. Mothers sometimes welcome this unexpected incursion because of the "empty-nest" syndrome of middle age. The adult child may be a divorced son or daughter, often bringing a child or two for the grandparents to baby-sit. It can be an adult child who found that living alone was more expensive than anticipated. After all, free room and board and laundry service aren't to be sneezed at.

So entire families are suffering from this modern displacement. Parents feel put upon and crowded out of their homes. The grown children become youngsters again to be bossed around. Often much dissension and unhappiness develop. Ministers' offices are beseiged with embattled middle-aged parents seeking advice on a new problem when they had expected to be looking forward to retirement.

Women who follow their husbands around the country on recurring corporate transfers also feel displaced. The couple gets settled, joins a church, begins to make friends, establishes business contacts in the community, and then are uprooted and on the move again. Some couples react defensively by making no close ties. Others form some and cling to them after they leave, unhappy at each successive and often abrupt move.

Then there are the families who move with servicemen

from post to post, state to state, and even country to country. The clergyman's family in some denominations often feels displaced, transferring from church to church, never knowing where the parent may be assigned next. Clergymen's children often form few close friends because of the shifts.

To sum up, many individuals suffer displacement from varying causes. I have moved from various areas of the United States and had to develop aids for handling this problem, as have friends and relatives. Hardly any one of us has not encountered displacement. The days of many generations of families being rooted in one place are gone forever. The world is in a state of flux.

The apostle Paul counsels us to be content in whatever state we are in (Phil. 4:11-12). The Diaspora was the scattering of the Jews in the Old Testament. God had a divine purpose in mind for His chosen people then. The same applies to Christians today. He wants us to make the best of our dwelling place and to emphasize the positive aspects. Even if one is temporarily located, one can make acquaintances and establish communication with neighbors. Even a short stay in a locality can produce long-lasting effects and friendships that endure. It is a shame to make a congenial acquaintance and then drop the person because of a move. It takes effort, though, to maintain ties. Writing letters occasionally can keep friends in touch. One has to keep the lines of communication open if one prizes a friendship. Visit when you are in the area. Of course, don't drop in without notice, suitcases in hand, expecting to be welcomed. Let your friend know when you will be in town or call when you arrive. If the time is inconvenient for a visit, you'll soon find out. A friend is always considerate and doesn't impose on good will or hospitality.

If you find yourself displaced, get acquainted with your neighbors as soon as possible. Find the local library, always one of my first contacts when I make a move. Read up on the local history. I enjoy seeking out old cemeteries and reading the tombstone inscriptions. Find out all you can about the place you are presently living. Take a local newspaper. It will give you something to talk about to new acquaintances and shows you are interested in your new home.

If no one calls on you within a short while, introduce yourself to people, especially longtime residents if you meet any. Let them know you are new to the community and are looking for a good, gospel-believing church, reliable merchants, and trustworthy professionals. Old-timers love to give sought or unsought advice on such matters. Listen flatteringly and follow the advice if at all possible. Let the person know later that you liked the person or store recommended to you.

My husband was transferred to a city in New England. Having been reared in easygoing Indiana where everybody talks to everybody, I found New Englanders distant and slow to respond to smiles and attempts at friendliness. I stood at a bus stop each morning with the same group, and no one spoke. Finally, in desperation, I commented to one woman about the weather, and we struck up a conversation. Even though my neighbors were not particularly cordial at first, I finally made friendships and still hear from those friends thirty years later. "A man that hath friends must shew himself friendly: and there is a friend that sticketh closer than a brother" (Prov. 18:24).

On the other hand, it is wise to beware of forming too quick intimacies when displaced, such as having neighbors drinking coffee in your kitchen every morning or socializing with the same couple every Saturday night. This pattern can backfire, and you may get trapped in a friendship you can't withdraw from gracefully without hurt feelings. Be warm and receptive, but form friendships slowly. One has to draw a subtle line between overquick commitments and none at all. It is like relishing one chocolate rather than stuffing down a whole pound at one sitting.

By all means, keep personal affairs to yourself. Some people tend to talk too freely to casual acquaintances and then wish they had been more discreet. One can hear startling revelations in a beauty shop. Discussing a husband's little faults and petty vices with everyone isn't too wise either.

Those tales may travel back to his employer. Men have lost jobs from a wife's loose tongue and lack of discretion. Be wary of intimate confidences unless you know the other person is absolutely trustworthy.

When you are displaced, do visit a church immediately. You meet the finest people in the world inside church walls. If there isn't one of your own denomination, visit around until you find a church that pleases you. Don't float forever, though. Some newcomers visit churches for months and never get established in one, thus making no Christian friends or commitment. One woman had attended our church off and on for eighteen years and finally decided to join the membership. Join a church or have your membership transferred even though you don't know how long you may stay in the area. Then you have a pastor to call upon in times of need, and you will more quickly get acquainted among the membership. You are now a part of a church family. "There is one body, and one Spirit, . . . One God and Father of all, who is above all, and through all, and in you all" (Eph. 4:4-6).

Establish important family traditions no matter where or how you are living. It is important to have familiar little niceties to cling to, a few precious items you've always carried with you. In my early marriage, we lived in a minuscule apartment for a while. We set up a tiny, artificial Christmas tree with five stiff branches that my parents had given us. We used it yearly until it fell apart. It was a symbol of home and families far away.

Because we had both enjoyed an ample Sunday dinner at home in the dining room, I cooked one on my rusty, three-burner stove and served it proudly on my best china on the little kitchen table. Following family traditions and establishing pleasant new ones keeps a couple from feeling disoriented every time exterior surroundings are changed. They make your dwelling a home no matter where it is or how humble it may be.

Barbara Cartland, the English romance novelist, tells in her autobiography of her own dauntless mother. She made her children dress up for dinner even when their circumstances were not of the best. She insisted they follow the dignified traditions that she had grown up with and would never allow her children to be uncouth or sloppy. In the up-and-down circumstances of her later life, Mrs. Cartland established the same patterns and surrounded herself with bright colors and pretty objects. She still is identified with the color pink and has made it her trademark.

When you're far away, write often to the folk back home. Mothers tell me sadly of sons and daughters who don't write for weeks on end. We all know how it hurts to watch for letters that rarely arrive. True, many prefer to use the telephone, but something about a quick call doesn't replace a warm, newsy letter one can reread over and over. Hardly anyone is too busy to write a weekly letter of at least a page, when one equates that with the average family watching television fifty hours a week.

When I lived miles from my family, I wrote them at least twice a week, my parents-in-law once a week, and was working full-time as well as keeping up a home and doing church work. And my parents were equally faithful to write. How I looked forward to those letters when I was far away and homesick, for they kept me informed on everyday happenings at home.

One hears of servicemen overseas and veterans in hospitals who never receive letters from families. I talked with such servicemen in the local veterans' hospital. Some had not heard from families in several years or had a visit. One wonders how relatives can be so heartless and indifferent to loved ones, especially to men who served their country loyally. "Remember them that are in bonds, as bound with them; and them which suffer adversity, as being yourselves also in the body" (Heb. 13:3).

Visits back home can be brief or prolonged, but limits must be understood ahead of time as to how long and if one is welcome for two weeks with four young children, a dog, a cat, and a canary. Being displaced doesn't give one carte blanche to impose on relatives for days on end, expecting entertainment like visiting royalty. Some family visitors do not offer to help with housework or to pay any of the expenses. A steak contributed to a meal or entertaining the hosts at a restaurant helps compensate for the extra work and expense of having visitors.

Sons and daughters are prone to pile in for holidays, bringing extra guests without warning, convinced that good old Mom loves to prepare dinner for twenty and to clean up afterward while the guests lounge in the family room. Because we live far away and come but seldom is no excuse not to help, or to invite our loved ones to come to our house occasionally for holidays. Parents should not be expected to always provide the holiday meals.

I talked with one middle-aged woman who had reared four children and said she had never cooked a holiday dinner for her family. The family of six had always gone to one of the mothers' homes. I couldn't help wondering if those grandmothers might not have enjoyed just once sitting down and being served themselves. No one wants to be known as a freeloader, and that applies in families as well as to outsiders.

Displacement need not break ties or strain them, but we have to work harder to keep them alive than if we see people frequently or live nearby. Joseph's story in the Old Testament is a good example of displacement and what glory he made out of his unsought and undesirable circumstances. Another is Paul's long confinement in a Roman prison where he consistently witnessed to his faith and won converts even among the jailers.

The Book of Ruth is a classic, inspiring story of a displaced woman who loved her mother-in-law Naomi and remained faithful to her in a foreign land. "And Ruth said, Entreat me not to leave thee, or to return from following after thee: for whither thou goest, I will go; and where thou lodgest, I will lodge: thy people shall be my people, and thy God my God" (Ruth 1:16).

A cheerful and uncritical attitude toward a new location and finding the positive elements in it are all-important to one's well-being. No matter where we live or how many times we move, we can welcome the new experience, broaden our knowledge of the world, and become more tolerant of others' values and cultures. Most importantly, as Christians, we can testify to our faith wherever we are. The Lord puts us in a place because He wants us to function in it as His representative. "Let your light so shine before men, that they may see your good works, and glorify your Father which is in heaven" (Matt. 5:16).

Even an elderly, ill, displaced person can be a lighthouse in the nursing or retirement home. One can impress the aides, nurses, doctors, and visitors with a sweet spirit and unwavering trust in God's providence. Sometimes visitors come away blessed from a contact with this kind of patient soul and feel they were ministered to equally.

12
Social Forces

"He that findeth his life shall lose it: and he that loseth his life for my sake shall find it" (Matt. 10:39).

We Christians must never, never forget the suffering caused by the Holocaust. Too many evangelicals now say, "Let's forget the past. Why dig all that up now?"

The horrifying statistics of the Holocaust are now too well documented for denial. Too many eyewitnesses can testify to what happened for the facts to be lightly dismissed as exaggerated. Our own United States forces saw the pitiful survivors when they liberated camps like Buchenwald and Dachau. The heartache of those who saw whole families exterminated is still fresh and poignant forty years later.

Many excellent books have been written exclusively on this dreadful subject, and it is not my purpose to duplicate what they say. But as a concerned layperson I must include in this book the tremendous mass suffering caused by dictators, wars, revolutions, and wretched social conditions. "And the Lord said unto Cain, Where is Abel thy brother? And he said, I know not: am I my brother's keeper?" (Gen. 4:9).

Our cities are teeming with the homeless of all ages and both sexes. Many have been evicted from their homes. Some are former mental patients released to fend for themselves. All over the world refugees flee from oppressive regimes or are barely existing in squalid refugee camps. Some Christians are presently involved in illegal sanctuary movements. In our country we are still struggling with problems left from our former heartless treatment of the Indians.

Millions live in communist countries where they are voiceless creatures of the state and cannot worship God as they choose. Bibles have to be hidden and cannot be purchased except surreptitiously. Hordes are starving because of the mishandling of tremendous aid programs and the inability of their governments to establish stable economies in Third World countries. All over the world, wars of long duration are being waged where it is almost impossible for residents to lead normal lives. Irish children have grown up never knowing a time of peace.

We Christians abide in an immoral, frightening world dominated by the forces of Satan. We need to remember, though, that Christ's times were similar. Every age has had its scourges, disasters, repressions, injustices, and mistreatment of common people. The fresh, inspirational message of Christ came to a cynical, paganistic world where most had given up hope for a Messiah to lead them out of oppression. "He was in the world, and the world was made by him, and the world knew him not" (John 1:10).

Today's Christian woman cannot hide her well-coiffured head in the sand, go to luncheons and teas advocating causes, drop a dollar bill in a basket, and dismiss the world's pain with a satisfied feeling she has done her duty. Today's Christian man cannot salve his conscience by lending his name to good causes and writing a check, but not be willing to take a stand or speak out on moral issues.

We see clearly what happened in Europe during the persecution of the Jews, Czechs, and other subjected people during World War II. To our eternal discredit, few Christians, even pastors, spoke out or attempted to help their persecuted neighbors even when they could have in subtle or hidden ways. Some Christians went into deserted houses of former Jewish friends and confiscated their belongings. They turned their heads when they saw Jews being humiliated and beaten in the streets. After the war, they lied by saying they knew nothing of what the Nazis were doing.

On the other hand, we have the glowing example of Corrie ten Boom and her brave little family in Holland, a few courageous priests and nuns in Italy, the residents of a whole village in southern France who sheltered their Jewish brothers and sisters and helped them escape. A few Protestant clergymen in Germany like Dietrich Bonhoeffer spoke out bravely against the Nazis and died in concentration camps for their defiance. His prison letters are a magnificent document of man's inhumanity to man and the triumph of the spirit over the forces of evil.

But generally and shamefully, the Christian churches and individual Christians stood silent and unprotesting in the face of Hitler's tyranny. In some instances they cooperated fully and openly with the regime. The treatment by Christian Poles of their Jewish compatriots is a sad indictment of Christians as a whole. They were as cruel as the Nazi invaders. So we can never dismiss the horrors resulting from the Holocaust. As Christians, we must resolve that they shall never happen again.

In the days when women rarely dared speak out on civil issues, Helen Hunt Jackson had the temerity to write of the United States government's mistreatment of the Indians. Her romantic novel *Ramona* and her nonfiction book *A Century of Dishonor* are the classic accounts of the injustice. These books spoke poignantly of the Indians' suffering in being moved off their lands into reservations. We are still reaping a bitter harvest from the mistakes made with our Indian brothers.

Another woman who defied injustice was Mother Jones, a famous labor leader who staunchly confronted the Colorado coal operators when the miners and their families were being treated like peons. Harriet Tubman, a black woman, helped slaves escape through the underground railroad before the Civil War. Their examples should inspire women everywhere to be a powerful force in standing for the right.

Christians of both sexes today are taking strong stands against unlimited abortion on demand, for equal rights for women in the marketplace, or against widespread pornography, and are speaking out on political and social issues all over the world. Our American author John Steinbeck, through his novels about the downtrodden, brought the plight of the migrant workers and others of the laboring class to the attention of the world.

However, far too many of us in our comfortable, placid lives prefer shutting our eyes to the world's suffering. We give feeble excuses such as "What can I do? I'm only one person," or "It gives me a headache to think about unpleasant subjects," or "I don't want to get involved." Worst of all is the statement, "A spiritual Christian ought to be above politics." These are all merely alibis to keep ourselves unsoiled and aloof from the problems and pain others have to face. "For this is the message that ye heard from the beginning, that we should love one another" (1 John 3:11).

Women with loving, protective husbands have difficulty empathizing with a lone woman struggling to support children or with the unmarried living alone. When we are contented and happy, we rarely are concerned with the pains of others until we are faced with trouble ourselves. Men who are suddenly out of work find themselves ignored by friends who are prosperous and secure in their jobs.

Many happy couples have been blindly unconcerned about the plights of lonely men and women in their churches until they themselves lose a spouse. Then they suddenly wake up to what it means to live alone. We plug up our ears to the strident cries of suffering everywhere. We need not be militant, carrying picket signs and shouting slogans in the streets if that is not our style, but we can take our stand against a social evil like pornography. We can refuse to patronize stores that openly market pornographic material and tell the manager why. We can write letters to companies and boycott products that support trashy and immoral television programs.

We can offer to help that pregnant girl whose lover or husband has walked out on her. We can stand up for good morals and influences in our communities and make our voices heard. Yes, we shall meet opposition and ridicule, but God's people have always had to face persecution. "Marvel not, my brethren, if the world hate you" (1 John 3:13).

Christianity has always been essentially a one-to-one religion. We make our main impact through individuals, not through the large evangelistic meetings, although these serve a purpose and have their place. It is the one-to-one, face-to-face witness to outsiders and the unchurched that counts in the long run. New church members often testify that they came to the church through the influence or invitation of one co-worker, one Christian neighbor, one friend who prayed for them.

We can't minister personally to the world's hurting masses except through large-scale charities or government aid, but we can help to lessen individual hurting when we find it close to home. All we have to do is look around us with open eyes at our city streets and even in our affluent communities. Our suburban church recently cooked over four hundred Thanksgiving dinners for our township alone. Names were supplied by social and welfare workers. We could hardly believe there were that many to be served where most inhabitants are well clothed and well housed.

We dress up in our finery to go to expensive luncheons in exclusive hotels and discuss world hunger while we nibble on delicacies. We Christians talk about evangelizing the unsaved throughout the world and fail to welcome the shy Vietnamese or Black who timidly slips into the back row of our sanctuary. We don't bother to nod to the unfamiliar person who occupies the pew beside us. Is it any wonder that those judging us Christians accuse us of blatant hypocrisy?

At one time in another state, I was involved with a church-supported coffeehouse and worked in the kitchen one evening a week. All kinds of young people dropped in to partake of the nonalcoholic refreshments, to play their guitars and sing, and to socialize. It was, of course, an evangelistic mission in a small rented building on a village street. Our patrons passed the word, and we had many visitors and regulars from surrounding towns. We workers considered it a resounding success and proudly reported back to the church board the progress we were making.

We on the staff subtly witnessed to our patrons. We were

trying particularly to win for Christ the members of a tough, raucous motorcycle gang who came in frequently. Finally, we did persuade three of them to attend the Sunday morning service. I doubt if any of them had ever been inside a church before.

The following week I watched them clanking down the aisle in their black leather jackets, still sporting their motorcycle chains and spurred boots. The usher unwisely led them to seats in a front pew where they must have felt conspicuous. But I thought, Glory be! We've won them to the Lord! I thought proudly of Christ's parable of the ninety and nine sheep and the one lost sheep.

After the service we from the coffeehouse staff rushed up to shake hands with our motorcycle friends. But most well-dressed members pointedly ignored them and brushed on by. Sad to say, I never saw them in church again. What a golden opportunity the congregation missed, for those three brave ones might have brought in the others in the gang. They undoubtedly were intimidated by the mink and sable coats and the cool, unfriendly glances in their direction. Even the minister didn't seem too glad to greet them.

Isn't it too bad how our Christian churches cause hurt by the way we subtly or openly exclude the different and socially unacceptable, as if we were operating an exclusive country club? As if one had to pass an acceptance test to sit in a pew? And yet Christ Himself chose to sup with obvious sinners and lepers and enjoined us to go out into the streets and bring in the poor outcasts to eat at our table.

No doubt we Christians deserve much of the criticism we receive. On the other hand, our critics fail to realize that it was Christ who first awarded dignity to women in a completely male-dominated society where women were considered no more than chattel. Some of His first converts were women, like the businesswoman Lydia, seller of purple, and Mary of Magdala, reputedly a former harlot. In Christianity there is no male or female. In some world religions even today, women are considered inferior creatures with no civil rights.

It is Christianity that has established hospitals, orphanages, schools, and nursing homes throughout the world where other religions have generally ignored the plight of the needy. For example, witness the wretched masses in India and how little has been done to help them except by compassionate Christians like Mother Teresa.

It was Christians through missions who freed the jungle savages from pantheism, a religion in which objects of nature are worshiped. The ignorant and superstitious lived in abject fear of evil spirits existing in everything around them. Christianity has been the only solace to mass sufferers. What else can sustain them except to look forward to God's promise that one day they will dwell in heaven with their Lord?

Some of the most glorious Christians I have met were in Protestant churches in Haiti, where dire poverty plagues the people. Their staunch faith sustains the Haitians when they have little else. Yet they sing the great hymns so meaningfully in their French Creole that they bring tears to the eyes. In a poor, repressive regime like Haiti, the Christian church is an important mission.

There I visited a hospital for the indigent maintained by the government in which the dying were stretched out on the floor on rags. Their relatives had to bring food to them. There were no screens on the open windows, and flies buzzed around their faces. It was a most pathetic sight. This is going on in a country where a former dictator's wife chartered an airplane to take her and her friends to Paris on extravagant shopping jaunts. But Christian organizations like World Vision are feeding the street orphans and the poor. I saw this great work being done throughout the island. Haitians are witnesses for the Lord in a land dominated by voodoo.

In recent events, we have witnessed a hostage airline pilot testifying that his faith had kept him calm facing the brutality of his captors. We have had the testimony of former prisoners of war, who, when placed in solitary confinement to break down their resistance, kept sane by repeating Scripture verses memorized as children in Sunday School. Martin Luther's "A Mighty Fortress Is Our God" has been a favorite hymn throughout the ages for those suffering through inquisitions, tortures, and imprisonment for political beliefs.

In a Greek-speaking Protestant church in Athens, Greece, I sat beside a young woman who spoke English. I told her I was an American. Even though I could not understand the sermon, I enjoyed the service and the hymns. At the end of the service, she slipped a few notes in my hand. She had outlined the sermon in English, so I would know what I had heard. I have found a common bond among Christians no matter what the language or the place.

In Scotland, when I visited a historic church, I was invited by the minister's wife to their apartment for tea on Sunday afternoon. I took advantage of the cordial invitation, found my way there on the bus, and was welcomed by the elderly couple. They were interested to hear of our adult Sunday School classes and our regular evening services, something rarely heard of in the old world. They deplored the fact that regular attendance in their churches had fallen off for all services.

Whenever I travel, I visit churches everywhere and enjoy worshiping with fellow Christians. I am sorry to write that the church is declining in the British Isles and especially in France and Sweden. Missionaries returning from these countries report widespread apathy and loss of membership. Europe has thus become a major mission field for American Protestantism since World War II, when people were left disillusioned and cynical after the enormous destruction.

In summary, for those hurting and caught in depressing social forces, the important point to remember is that God never deserts us no matter what the environment. He promises He will never let His own be plucked from His hand by any foe. As a hostage, victim of injustice, or refugee, we can cling to His promises. He will supply our basic needs and give us new life, but not necessarily all our selfish wants. And we need to do all we can to help the unfortunate people in our own communities and throughout the world.

"Open thy mouth, judge righteously, and plead the cause of the poor and needy" (Prov. 31:9).

13
Loss of Faith

"If then God so clothe the grass, which is to-day in the field, and to-morrow is cast into the oven; how much more will he clothe you, O ye of little faith?" (Luke 12:28).

Of all the hurts that one can undergo, the loss of faith is surely the most poignant and significant. And this particular hurt is self-imposed. We can't lay the blame on anyone else. This one is between God and us alone.

It is apparent that even the strongest Christian can waver at times when despondent and wonder if God is still there and if He is listening. We ordinary people think ashamedly that we must be the only ones who ever questioned our faith. The mighty Book of Job in the Old Testament is a statement of God's testing the faith of one servant. The saints prayed continuously for their faith to be strengthened. Even Peter, "the Rock," ran away the night before Christ's crucifixion and denied Him three times, as Jesus had predicted he would.

We see many instances of lost faith, temporarily or permanently. Young people reared in Christian families and in good churches leave for college, are exposed to secular and even atheistic professors, and decide organized religion is no longer for them. They either lose their faith altogether or become involved in a dangerous cult that is not centered in Christ but in a strong leader.

Young married couples become engrossed in furthering careers, establishing homes, and starting families, and the church sees them no more. When all is going well, they decide they no longer need the bulwark of religion. That's for older people, they decide, who have no more exciting things to think about, or for children in Sunday School.

Successful middle-agers are convinced they have it made, for they have reached the pinnacle of professions. They are self-made people, forgetting that God is the essence of good and that they are dependent on Him for even the air they breathe. Besides God, many others have helped them along the way. They are now socially active civic leaders. What do they need with prayer, a crutch to lean on? Just the weak and unsuccessful have to call on supernatural forces for help. If they can't make a splash elsewhere, they can be frogs in a little puddle and feel self-important in a small church.

The old have grown weary of prolonged well-doing. They have worked faithfully in a church for years, sacrificed financially for it, and finally decide, What's the use? Is it worth it? I've done my share and nobody cares. No one appreciates me any more. I'm too old to be of any use now. And if God valued my service, would He have brought all those troubles on me I've had to bear?

Then there are those who have sinned greatly, who become overcome with guilt and remorse and drop out of the fellowship. They think everyone surely knows of their terrible sins and are ashamed and embarrassed. They know the church roof would topple in if they showed up on Sunday morning. Wouldn't all those perfect saints in the pews scorn them?

The dread disease affecting all the forenamed is called loss of faith. The question inevitably arises: Did they ever have a genuine faith, a sincere commitment, to begin with? If they fall away so easily, was there ever any depth of belief?

It is never our place as Christians to judge the sincerity of another's faith. Only God can do that. He alone knows the heart. But we can decide what we ourselves must do to hold on to our faith, to help those who have wavered or fallen away, and to strengthen our churches to meet the needs of the hurting. If we are honest, we must admit that frequently we Christians don't meet the hurts of those who most need help. Thus we lose them. We either ignore their silent pleas or serve up platitudes with no depth of compassion and empathy. We even make them feel guilty when they most need love and uncritical attention and not further condemnation. They may already be loathing themselves with heavy doses of self-condemnation.

Nothing can affect our lives so greatly as to be lost to the family of God. The one unpardonable sin is to deny Christ. "Wherefore I say unto you, All manner of sin and blasphemy shall be forgiven unto men: but the blasphemy against the Holy Spirit shall not be forgiven unto men" were Christ's own words (Matt. 12:31).

God never loses sight of His own, regardless of our heedless actions and choices to forget Him. We may be out of fellowship for a time, but God receives us back with open arms when we wish to return. The parables of the prodigal son and the one lost sheep both vividly illustrate this lesson. "He that believeth on him is not condemned: but he that believeth not is condemned already, because he hath not believed in the name of the only begotten Son of God" (John 3:18).

Disappointment in God is a universal problem among believers. If we do not receive prompt and favorable answers to our prayers, we are convinced that God has lost interest in us. If we endure a crushing disappointment, we tend to blame God, even though the hurt may have been brought on by our own folly or someone else's close to us. It is human nature to look for somewhere else to cast blame, and who better than God? Since God foreordains what is to happen to us, then it must be His fault when something bad comes. In our misery we curse God as Job's wife advised him to do (Job 2:9).

One of the most disheartening experiences one can have is to try to talk with a person who either has completely lost his faith or is convinced that a just God does not exist. When a person most should lean on God's care and providence is often the very time that one becomes most embittered with Him. "Therefore I say unto you, Take no thought for your life, what ye shall eat, or what ye shall drink; . . . Is not the life more than meat, and the body more than raiment?" (Matt. 6:25).

We have all experienced attending the funeral of a former Christian who fell away from the church, or of one who never professed any belief. We are left wondering what hope the family has or what they are leaning on in their grief. What can one conscientiously say in comfort? It is too late then to pray a person into heaven. One must have made that choice to accept Christ on one's own. God has no grandchildren, only children.

Successive disappointments and hurts *can* cause a person to reel and turn away from a life of faith. Disappointments in people cause us to become disheartened, cynical, and cold. When those we love disillusion us, we often blame God for their dereliction. Not only are we cut off from humans in this situation, but we turn away from God's love that never fails us when all else does.

One of the most intelligent men I know claims no religious belief. He was brought up in Sunday School and had a devout Christian mother. When he became a teenager, he began to question what he had been taught. By the time he was an adult, he had become an agnostic. He states that he believes in nothing or no one, for he long ago lost his trust in human nature. What hurts bring a person to this state? What disappointment causes a person to look upon everyone with distrust? What code or philosophy can such a person cling to? What hope can one have for his life? How does one look upon death? There is no hope ever to meet his loved ones again in an afterlife.

The biographies of Malcolm Muggeridge and C. S. Lewis, both eminent English writers, are worth reading for those who have lost their faith. Both men tell how empty and meaningless their lives were until they experienced a religious awakening and how much richer their lives have become. The American writer Eugenia Price described the difference in her life after she came to believe in Christ. Those who have lost their faith or never had one find that when all human resources and other persons fail them, they have nothing left to shore them up. All is lost, and there is nowhere else to turn. It is often said that at this point when we fall to our knees, we then turn to God.

The Christian lives with a joy and peace of mind that continues in spite of circumstances, disappointments, hurts, and the unjust blows of fate. Christians know that nothing can separate them from the love of God, for He has told them so.

How can the present-day church help those who are hurting from loss of faith? Argument or haranguing will not do it, but only tender *agape* love and the willpower to listen with an uncritical attitude and a concern for the other individual. Nothing succeeds like the quiet, sincere person who is willing to help whenever possible. A lending of Christian books sometimes works, although one should not deluge anyone with material to be read. The Christian who forces tracts on those unwilling to read them is being discourteous.

We never know when a seed planted will sprout. Sometimes it takes years. We have to learn patience. People have been brought back to the fellowship after years of absence because of the faithful friendship and prayers of one Christian. Adults nostalgically remember childhood Sunday School teachers years afterward. Those who fall away often return to the church when a tragedy hits, and the church people rally around. A listening ear is one of the greatest gifts we can bring to those out of fellowship. Sometimes they merely need someone to talk to who will be discreet. Men in pain will come to a trusted pastor only as a last resort when everything else has failed. They are ashamed to admit their hurts to anyone else.

A terrible void exists when God is shut out of one's life. Most of us have gone through periods when He has seemed far away, or we could not feel His presence. We cannot depend on feelings, though. In this instance we must rely on our previous knowledge.

I believe that miracles are happening all around us today, not in the ordinary, natural events but in those outside the normal physical realm that have no other explanation. We all have read of miraculous healings brought about by fervent prayer. God can do anything He chooses and will do that which is within His will and purpose for us.

So we can help those who are hurting from loss of faith by our personal testimonies of God's goodness in our lives and in others' lives. I am not referring to the type of testimony that one dedicated missionary gave. She started with when she was six years old, went through each succeeding year, and told how God had influenced both major and minor decisions. At the time she must have been forty years old. By the end of the long odyssey, most listeners had slipped out. Those who were left surely wondered why God had not counseled her on how not to exhaust an audience!

We have to beware of reciting the thrilling testimonies—to us—that only convince the lost that Christians are bores. We do relish our place in the sun, and some of us seize every opportunity to shine. You all know the person I mean, the one who rises in every prayer meeting to recite the same story again—and again. By such lack of consideration for others, we merely center attention on ourselves, not on God's faithfulness.

Some churches send out members to call on the backslidden and to talk to them about coming back into the fellowship. I believe a mistake is made sending several armed with Bibles and canned speeches. Nothing intimidates a confused, hurting person more than to open the door and find four well-meaning persons waiting to guide him back from the primrose path. I heard of one case when the unannounced delegation arrived at 9:00 PM. Any wonder they were not greeted very cordially? We need to be sensitive, courteous, and diplomatic to those who have dropped out of the fellowship. These people are already on the defensive. Nobody wants to be reprimanded or treated like an errant child. A spirit of love and kindness is all-important.

I'll sum up this chapter with a Scripture passage I have found meaningful in my own life and a good one to leave with those hurting from loss of faith. "Take therefore no thought for the morrow: for the morrow shall take thought for the things of itself. Sufficient unto the day is the evil thereof" (Matt. 6:34).

Conclusion

If you have read through this book and reached this point, you should have arrived at certain conclusions. I hope you have, but if not, I'll enumerate some ideas I intended to illustrate to the best of my ability. Most of them you already know, but they bear repetition.

Life is a struggle against the forces of evil for all of us, regardless of status or place, and hurt and disappointment are inevitable. We need all the help and strength we can get. We are admonished to be kind to one another, tenderhearted, forgiving, and bearing each other's infirmities. Whether we are young or old, handsome or homely, we face the reality of eventual heartache. I know this is a sobering prospect and one we dislike confronting at any age.

When we are young, energetic, and attractive, the world is our oyster just waiting to be pried open. We confidently believe *we* shall never face those dreary problems that beset our parents and made them irritable. *Our* lives will be different. *We'll* avoid all those foolish errors our elders made. *We* won't be possessed by materialism and always grubbing for a dollar. *We'll* make successful marriages and careers. *We* won't allow any bickering in our model homes. *We* intend to watch our weight, our health, and our career choices. *We* won't be trapped in a routine, meaningless existence working to pay bills as older generations were.

But natural disasters do occur, unforeseen circumstances swamp us, jobs suddenly vanish, weight creeps up unnoticed, gray hairs and wrinkles duly appear. With a combination of irony, humor, and regret, we find ourselves trapped in the very situations we swore in our youth to avoid! With the generosity we didn't always grant to our parents, we tell ourselves we couldn't control the fates. It's not our fault we've fallen into a morass and gotten stuck there.

As Robert Burns so aptly stated in his poem "To a Mouse": "The best laid schemes o' mice and men, Gang aft agley." When I taught this poem, students always announced how they had their lives planned. Listening with a smile, I stopped myself from disillusioning them at their tender age. While goals are necessary for inspiration, life *can* crash in when we least expect or deserve it.

In short, if we are prudent, we had better start early building our inner foundations to meet the hurts that are bound to come in one form or another. Delaying until they envelop us like a cloak is too late. Those who do, believing they are exempt from disaster, are the very ones who are seen in psychiatrists' waiting rooms. A firm grasp of biblical principles, a memorization of Scriptures, an allegiance to a good church, Christian friends—all these are mighty bulwarks to the hurting everywhere.

As I was working on this book, a plane disaster occurred in which 250 soldiers returning at Christmastime were killed. When a grieving young wife was being interviewed before the television camera, she cried hysterically, "These things happen to other people! Not to me! I don't want it to be me!" Her anguished reaction was typical of all of us. We never expect that we shall be the recipient of the sudden tragedy. We can be easily philosophical and remote toward others' griefs, yet when it is we ourselves, how different the situation becomes. We are just as crushed as everyone else in similar circumstances.

In addition, memorized verses and Bible study must be supplemented by concrete action. Too many nominal Christians know the doctrines and can recite the confession and prayers by heart, but that's as far as their energies and interests go. Emphasis is placed on individual spirituality and piety, but this overemphasis on personal piety alone is not compatible with Christ's teaching and example. "If any man serve me, let him follow me; and where I am, there shall also my servant be: if any man serve me, him will my Father honour" (John 12:26).

We pray for our souls' salvation and those of our friends and relatives, but we are firmly commanded to act out our concern and compassion for our fellow pilgrims on this grim planet. *Christian love is shown by doing.* This lesson is reiterated in all of Christ's teaching and parables.

This question confronts thinking Christians. Why do many of those faithful attenders at Bible studies shun coming to give comfort at mortuaries, hospital rooms, and with the homebound? They adopt the stances of spirituality, extol the minister's sermons, and yet lose sight of the supreme goal of our study—to serve one's fellow human beings to the utmost and to forget oneself in the doing. The Lord emphasized the lowly servant concept by washing feet Himself. True, He looks upon our hearts, but we are warned that He also evaluates our works. He expects us to be up and doing. We do not win salvation by those works, for that is conferred by God's grace and mercy to us. We can never strive hard enough to deserve mercy because no one's works are good enough. "For by grace are ye saved through faith; and that not of yourselves: it is the gift of God: Not of works, lest any man should boast" (Eph. 2:8-9).

Regardless of the depth of our own hurts, we must dare to venture out on the firing lines of life and help prop up the other stricken and fallen.

The farther we proceed in our Christian pilgrimage, the better able we are to withstand the successive blows of misfortune and God's discipline. Each new hurt we face and conquer gives us that much more stamina and confidence to withstand the next one. Courage builds renewed courage whenever we are tested. The mighty power that God imbues in His children never deserts us. That miraculous strength has been proved over and over in the lives of saints and martyrs, in our friends' lives, and in our own, if we have been faithful.

We shall not find good *in* every situation, but good can

result *from* it. Who can honestly say that a bout of painful shingles or a broken leg is good? Yet authors Catherine Marshall and Jessamyn West both tell in their autobiographies of how confinement in bed with tuberculosis caused them to begin writing. John Bunyan wrote his masterpiece *Pilgrim's Progress* while confined to the Bedford Jail. John Milton produced the epic *Paradise Lost* after he became totally blind. Robert Louis Stevenson developed his keen imagination for adventure tales when he was a sickly child. There are numerous other examples of how good came out of a less than perfect situation.

If we adopt the unconvincing stance that God brings only good to us and we must be thankful for the disasters, we are looked upon as foolish, and nobody pays the least attention to us. The woman with a pious smile and the syrupy voice is a mockery of the model woman. The man with the booming voice uttering clichés accompanied by a back slap merely turns people off. We never win anyone to Christ by insincerity. That is made clear in the parables. Paul taught us to give thanks *in* every situation, not *for* the unpleasant circumstances, and to keep our eyes fixed on Christ. He will see us through our valleys of despair and carry us on His shoulders as the shepherd does the lost sheep. The Lord brings good out of our hurts if we commit ourselves fully to His hands and let Him work in us and through us.

Patience is a virtue few of the young possess and not all of the old, but it is essential to overcome suffering. God answers all prayers in His way in His own time with yes, no, or wait. We want overnight solutions to fit our mode of life in which everything else is instantaneous. He simply does not work that way.

I recall a persistent prayer that was finally answered fourteen years later in a way least expected. I had long ago sullenly determined God was ignoring me and wasn't doing a single thing to help me. Now I can see through all those long, waiting years, He was working out that solution for me. Nor does He answer in the way we assumed He would. Sometimes we get a jolting surprise, for God, who has all attributes, also has a sense of humor. He sees the overall pattern of our lives, where we see only the unconnected single threads.

If we are praying for a truly heartfelt need, not just a luxurious or frivolous wish, He will meet it in some way for our own good. Don't be like the boy I taught in Sunday School who kept praying at the age of fourteen for a motorcycle. Needless to say, his anxious mother was not at all in favor of God's saying yes to that prayer, and He never did.

Webster's definition for *commit* is: "to put in charge or trust; deliver for safekeeping, to pledge; bind." This is what we mean when we commit ourselves to our Lord and Savior. We make ourselves pliable and willing to be led wherever He commands us, to do as He orders. We receive these directions through daily prayer, Bible reading, and the voice of the Holy Spirit dwelling within us. The old hymn that describes the potter modeling the clay is still apropos of the modern Christian. God never changes even though all else does in this world. He stands firm, the only Rock we can cling to when all else fails, and the waves of disaster splash over us as we hang on for dear life.

Christ never demands that we be successful or that we win, only that we be faithful to the very end. We must practice the virtue of gratitude, remembering that life is full of daily blessings. Out of the worst heartache and pain can come final victory. God compliments us by giving us burdens to carry.

The finest compliment that can be paid to anyone in a funeral eulogy is that he was a lifelong, dedicated Christian whose life was an inspiration to others. This supersedes all praise of good looks, intelligence, or civic position. Often it is pronounced over one who has suffered innumerable hurts and remained a radiant Christian to the end. We all know those heartaches will be healed in paradise when we meet our Lord face to face. All burdens are lifted at Calvary, and all tears are washed away.

So may your hurts be healed.

Suggested Further Reading

Allen, Charles L. *God's Psychiatry*. Old Tappan, N.J.: Fleming H. Revell Co., 1963.

Bonhoeffer, Dietrich. *Letters and Papers from Prison*. New York: Macmillan, 1953.

Guder, Eileen. *To Live in Love*. Grand Rapids: Zondervan Publishing House, 1957.

Lewis, C. S. *The Case for Christianity*. New York: Macmillan, 1968.

Little, Paul. *Know What You Believe*. Wheaton, Ill.: Victor, 1970.

_____. *Know Why You Believe*. Downers Grove, Ill.: Inter-Varsity Press, 1970.

Morrison, Frank. *Who Moved the Stone*. New York: Faber & Faber, 1930.

Muggeridge, Malcolm. *A Twentieth Century Testimony*. Nashville: Thomas Nelson, 1978.

Packer, J. I. *Knowing God*. Downers Grove, Ill.: Inter-Varsity Press, 1973.

Sheen, Fulton H. *Peace of Soul*. New York: McGraw-Hill Book Co., 1949.

Smedes, Lewis B. *Love Within Limits*. Grand Rapids: Wm. B. Eerdmans Publishing Co., 1978.

Smith, Hannah Whitall. *The Christian's Secret of a Happy Life*. Old Tappan, N.J.: Fleming H. Revell Co., 1974.

Stuart, James S. *The Wind of the Spirit*. Nashville: Abingdon Press, 1968.

Ten Boom, Corrie. *The Hiding Place*. New York: Guideposts, 1971.

Tournier, Paul. *The Healing of Persons.* New York: Harper & Row, 1965.

_____. *The Whole Person in a Broken World.* New York: Harper & Row, 1964.

Trueblood, Elton. *The Company of the Committed.* New York: Harper & Row, 1961.